Activities

for school-age child care

Rosalie Blau
Elizabeth H. Brady
Ida Bucher
Betsy Hiteshew
Ann Zavitkovsky
Docia Zavitkovsky

Photographs by

Jean Berlfein
9, 10, 12, 14, 19, 40, 44, 57, 73, 78

Children's Centers,
Santa Barbara School District
35 and 64

Craig Currier
18

Gail Ellison
60

Ellen Galinsky
45

John T. Harlan
70

Steve Herzog
54

James Seligman
28, 31, 56

Diane Wasserman
22, 42, 48, 50, 51, 61

Illustrations by
Caroline Taylor

Copyright © 1977. All rights reserved.

National Association for the Education of Young Children
1834 Connecticut Avenue, N.W.
Washington, DC 20009

Library of Congress Catalog Card Number : 77-91044

ISBN Catalog Number: 0-912674-57-1

Printed in the United States of America.

Activities

for
school-age
child
care

Rosalie Blau
Elizabeth H. Brady
Ida Bucher
Betsy Hiteshew
Ann Zavitkovsky
Docia Zavitkovsky

The National Association for the
Education of Young Children

What is needed for school-age children?

A center which can "become the focus of social and service programs, involving families, neighbors, local businesses, civic organizations, and any other agencies in the community" with "the responsibility of serving as a bridge to the larger community in which the child lives."

From "A Statement of Principles"
Office of Child Development
Department of Health, Education, and Welfare
Washington, D.C.
1971

Authors

Rosalie Blau
Consultant, Early Childhood Education Programs, Los Angeles, California.

Elizabeth H. Brady
Professor of Educational Psychology, California State University, Northridge.

Ida Bucher
Director, First Presbyterian Church School of Santa Monica, California.

Betsy Hiteshew
Director, Santa Monica College Child Development Center, Santa Monica, California.

Ann Zavitkovsky
Community Health Developer, Hano, Hawaii.

Docia Zavitkovsky
Director, Children's Centers and Preschool Education, Santa Monica, California,
Unified School District.

Preface

The Office of Child Development (OCD) and the Office of Economic Opportunity (OEO) grant #H – 9807, through Research for Better Schools, Ronald K. Parker, Principal Investigator, provided financial support in 1970 for developing a daily activity program for five- to ten-year-old children. The opinions expressed in the manuscript did not necessarily reflect the position or policy of OCD or OEO, and no official endorsement by these agencies should be inferred.

The original manuscript was expanded, enriched, and revised in 1977 to increase its relevance and usefulness to those living and working creatively with school-age children in day care programs.

We wish to give special thanks to Sue Bond and Cathy Atwood for their help in updating the bibliography and developing "suggested activity units"; to Beverly Lydiard for her invaluable editorial assistance; and to Diane Wasserman, James Seligman, and Jean Berlfein for their photography. We also wish to thank our typists, Thelma Caldwell and Jan MacGregor.

Rosalie Blau
Elizabeth H. Brady
Ida Bucher
Betsy Hiteshew
Ann Zavitkovsky
Docia Zavitkovsky

November 1977

Contents

1   Introduction

5   *Chapter 1.*   Daily Activities and Schedules

9   *Chapter 2.*   Routines: Ruts or Routes to Learning?

13   *Chapter 3.*   Active Play: Moving to Learn

19   *Chapter 4.*   Arts and Crafts

29   *Chapter 5.*   Blocks

33   *Chapter 6.*   Dramatic Play and Creative Dramatics

39   *Chapter 7.*   Puppets and Marionettes

43   *Chapter 8.*   Music and Dance

49   *Chapter 9.*   Stitchery, Weaving, and Knitting

55   *Chapter 10.*   Working with Wood

59   *Chapter 11.*   Water, Sand, and Mud

65   *Chapter 12.*   Cooking

71   *Chapter 13.*   Science, Nature, and Gardening

77   *Chapter 14.*   Community Resources

79   *Chapter 15.*   Staff Meetings: Toward an Effective Program

81   Index

84   Selected NAEYC Publications

Introduction

This is a working notebook on planning daily activities for school-age children during the hours when they are not in the classroom and not at home. In many communities across the United States, people like you are setting up or operating child care centers where children from five to ten years of age can receive the care that, for one reason or another, their families cannot give them.

The ideas and suggestions in this book have been developed by finding out what kind of care children need and what parents and guardians who place their children in centers want for them. Each program of care will be special and different in some ways, just as each child and each family the program serves will be special and different. Yet the child care centers, as well as the children and their families, will also have things in common. For instance, every child who comes to a child care center—

- needs care,

  BUT needs it for a particular reason.

- spends most of his or her time at the center with children approximately the same age,

  BUT at home may be an only child or one of many children.

- has a family to go home to at the end of the day,

  BUT that family may be different from others in size, members, and family relationships.

- comes from a home which taught certain things and expected certain behavior,

  BUT each home will have its own way and its own expectations; these may differ greatly.

- has interests, talents, habits, and values,

  BUT these may be similar to those of other children in the center or they may be very different.

- will behave in certain ways learned before coming to the center,

  BUT ways of behaving toward new things and people—being independent or dependent, brave or fearful, bold or shy with adults and children—will be unique to each child.

- has social and personal skills,

  BUT may not have learned skills and habits others take for granted.

- has personal qualities to which others respond and personal needs which should be met,

  BUT each child will have charm, strengths, and a special way of viewing the world that is unique to that child.

Children between the ages of five and ten may come to a children's center both before school for breakfast and after school. They may have been at school for three hours or more, probably five hours for the eight-, nine-, and ten-year-olds. When they come to a center, they will be looking for activities different from what has gone on in schools—just as they would if they were going home—so the pace will be different from the pace of school, more leisurely and often stretched over a longer period of time.

Elementary school-age children have developed interests and skills. They are capable of sustaining an interest in an activity if they are helped to deepen and extend their work and study. They like to attempt and to master things that are difficult. The unfamiliar is challenging, but they want to learn about it. They enjoy exploring a world which is ever-widening in both time and distance. A study of dinosaurs, for example, can entice eight-year-olds to want to build a scale model. As they research for information on what these animals ate, they begin to learn the relationship between eating habits and anatomic structures. Investigation of electronic communication from Citizen Band radios in cars and trucks to investigation of how instructions are communicated to Explorer digging on Mars could go on for months. Photography, animation, even motion pictures, are vehicles for exciting records of episodes in the children's own lives and the life of their neighborhood and school.

At this age friendships are forming. Jokes and fun with others are important. Clubs, passwords, and mystic signs and symbols attract. Small groups enjoy working together. There are also times when a child wants to be alone.

Children like to feel competent and be competent. The nine-year-old who says proudly that the model just completed is really *authentic* is creating standards for her own work. Children want to be expected to work carefully so they can feel pride in what they have done.

The rhythm of the program must take into account these desires to explore, reflect, expand, and complete in accordance with the rhythms of individual children's tempos and interests.

Parents or guardians who choose a school-age child care center for their five- to ten-year-olds do so for many reasons. If the center staff members are to provide what the parent wants, they must understand why the child has been placed in the center and what the parent hopes for, just as they must understand what each child needs and wants.

We have chosen brief sketches of three children—Joseph, Carrie, and Timothy—who are like many of those cared for in centers. As you read the sketches, you will see more clearly how important it is to find out the wants and needs and hopes of parents and children. Which children do you care for with similar (or different) wants and needs and expectations? How can you use this book to best serve the needs of these families?

THIS IS JOSEPH:

Joseph is eight years old, the middle child of five children who live with their grandmother, Mrs. J. She works as an aide at a convalescent home and has had most of the responsibility for her daughter's children ever since her son-in-law deserted the family. Her daughter, Mrs. T., got into several bad situations, but she works sometimes and has earned good money in the past.

Joseph is good at sports and games and not so good at school work. His report cards always show lots of F's and bad marks for conduct. At the center he is a "live wire."

Joseph is already beginning to play softball; he has learned from watching his older brothers and boys on their street. He can get a game organized and going at the center even with boys older than he is. In everything he does, he is strong, active, and energetic. He is naturally a leader with the younger children and seems happy at the center as long as there is lots to do outdoors and nobody asks him to do any school work.

Joseph has a quick temper; he gets in fights often, but once the fight is over he gets back his good nature. Joseph seems very independent. Still, there are times when he just wants to be around the assistant teacher at the center.

Joseph is always ready to help her with anything she asks and she finds it hard to understand why the teacher in school gives Joseph so many bad conduct marks. As far as she is concerned, he is just "all boy."

Joseph's Grandmother and Mother:

Joseph's mother is currently serving a term in a minimum security prison for cashing bad checks. This has upset Joseph's grandmother very much. Mrs. J. took the children to visit their mother on her birthday recently, but she pretended to the children that the prison was really a hospital. She wrote her daughter ahead of time not to walk around—just to sit and talk with them in the visitors' room—because she had told the children "something is wrong with mother's legs."

Mrs. J. is strict with the children, especially the boys. She has different ideas than her daughter about lots of things. When Mrs. T. learned that the school-age center would care for the children because she was on welfare, Mrs. J. didn't want them to go there. She felt that they could be on their own at home after school; she thought the neighbors would be critical of her for "not taking care of my own."

Mrs. T. told her mother that that was nonsense; there was no reason why the state shouldn't help take care of her family. Actually, Mrs. T. is pretty vague about how the center happens to be there and how it is financed; her social worker made the arrangements for her.

Mrs. T. is resentful toward lots of people, especially men. She finds it hard to deal with her three older children—all boys—although she enjoys her two youngest—both pretty girls. She likes to dress them up and take them out to windowshop or go to a movie. She thinks the boys can manage on their own since there is always a ball game or something like that going on in the street.

When she comes home, Mrs. T. thinks maybe she will go over to the center and get acquainted.

What about Joseph?

Is some of Joseph's bravado and independence a cover for feelings of loss and resentment?

Is Joseph bewildered by or angry at his grandmother's deceptions and the absence of his mother?

Is Joseph looking to the center staff for the loving neither his mother nor his grandmother can give him?

Can the center staff establish a liaison to help the teacher at school understand Joseph better?

Can the center program provide and enhance the opportunities for Joseph to continue success at sports, in leadership roles, in using his real skills and strengths?

And His Mother?

Can a supportive way be found to bring Joseph's mother into contact with other mothers?

Is she feeling her own mother's ambivalence and anger at having to shoulder responsibility?

Can she become interested in and supportive of her sons as well as her daughters?

THIS IS CARRIE:

Carrie, seven, is the oldest of three children whose mother died in childbirth three years ago. Her father, Mr. L., had hired a series of babysitters and housekeepers to care for Carrie and her two brothers, ages six and three. None stayed very long, and none seemed to satisfy Mr. L.; he noticed that the children didn't seem happy with any of them.

Mr. L. heard about the school-age child care center from the first grade teacher last year. When he learned about the program for prekindergarten children at the same center, he promptly enrolled all three children.

Mr. L. has a job in a company he has been with for seven years. The family income is steady but small. Carrie can do many things in the kitchen and around the house; she has always been a big help in taking care of her smaller brothers. The family has no relatives in the area. Neighbors are helpful and kind, but often the children's clothing goes unmended and shoes unrepaired.

When Carrie came to the center she was solemn, worrying aloud to the director about whether her little brother was all right in the preschool room. She was so capable that the director soon came to rely on her for organizing things, cleaning up, and helping other children.

But the director has noticed how often Carrie acts more like an adult than like a child. She doesn't giggle and fool around much but always keeps busy and helpful. She is a bright little girl; each report card time she proudly brings her good report to show the center staff.

Carrie's Father:

Mr. L. is a good-looking, rather thin and tense young man who clearly enjoys his children and is proud of them. Recently he confided to the center director that he and his wife had many dreams and plans for their children and that he wants to do his best to make those dreams come true. He is going to night school in hopes that some day he will finish a college degree and move to a better paying job. Before Mrs. L. died, they had a carefully laid out pattern for the next five years in which he would finish school and they would move to another part of the country; he had thought about becoming a teacher.

This plan has been slowed down because of his wife's death and all the extra responsibilities that has meant. Finding the center, Mr. L. says, is the one really wonderful thing that has happened to the family since then. He used to worry so much about Carrie "growing up too fast because she had to help me with the others." Until the family came to the center he didn't feel he had anyone to really talk to about the things he and his wife used to discuss—right ways of bringing up the children, how to help them do well in school, what were good books or toys to buy, the right clothes to dress them in, and things like that.

Now, Mr. L. never misses a parent meeting when such ideas are discussed. Also, he is willing to take time on weekends to build things at the center. Last week he finished a climbing structure for the preschool. Next week he is going to start on some bookshelves for Carrie's group.

Most important of all, Mr. L. says he feels that the children are safe and happy and getting the kind of guidance and example their mother would want them to have from the staff of the center.

What about Carrie?

Has so much responsibility at so early an age robbed Carrie of the chance to be spontaneous and free and sometimes dependent on others?

Does Carrie still need reassurance about the welfare of others in her family—perhaps her father as well as her brothers?

Is there a need for Carrie to move a little away from her family and toward other children her own age?

Does the center provide and reward lots of fun activities for children like Carrie?

Can the adults in the center provide Carrie with contacts in which she can learn to laugh and make jokes with grownups and depend on them to help her and love her?

Does the center have a liaison with community groups like Bluebirds, Brownies, and the YWCA or YMCA?

And Her Father?

Does Carrie's father need help in understanding the importance of values besides achievement and responsibleness?

Can he use the center's resources to learn more about normal child development?

THIS IS TIMOTHY:

Timothy has been coming to the center for two years since his mother had to find a place for him and his two younger brothers so that she could work full-time.

Timothy is eight years old and his brothers are six and five. He loves the center and, most of all, a college student named Mel who works at the center before and after classes. The split day means that Tim can see Mel first thing in the morning before school; he chatters away with Mel about his newly found interest in baseball. Mel is an athlete and can add to Tim's rapidly growing fund of information about sports and players.

In the late afternoon, Mel takes Tim and three or four other boys to a park to play ball with the children there. Several times Mel has picked up Tim on Saturdays to see a game or go to the YMCA to swim.

Tim is one of the children in the center who seems to move comfortably from home, to the center, to school, and back, taking in his stride all the different people and activities, having lots of interests, and fitting in well with other children at school, the center, or the park. He is a happy boy, affectionate toward his mother and his two brothers and Mel, but independent, too. Tim now helps cheerfully with putting away and cleaning up, although he didn't when he first came to the center. When he began to understand how many different things there were to do there and how many activities were going on at the center, Tim not only accepted routines but has been a big help in getting other chidren to do the "housekeeping" necessary to take care of equipment, games, and materials for so many children.

Timothy's Mother:

Mrs. B. is thirty years old; she supports her three children herself. Without the center, as she has often told the director, she couldn't do it. She would have to go on welfare or take her children back to her hometown to live with her family, which she didn't want to do.

She likes being independent and self-supporting. She thinks people should stand on their own feet and is bringing up her children to think the same way.

Mrs. B. is a college graduate, but she worked only briefly before she married and had her children. She was fortunate in getting a position with a company with opportunities for advancement; she takes full advantage of adult school classes and company training.

Not only is she grateful for the center's taking good care of her children, but she appreciates the fact that they do more. It is through Mel and the center that Tim is having a chance to grow in his love of sports and participate in games. The younger boys also are having chances to develop their interests. When she picks them up at six each day, all three boys usually seem happy, eager to talk about what they have been doing. Before Mrs. B. found the center, she would often come home to find that the boys had misbehaved (according to whatever sitter was there) and they, in turn, were often cross and overtired; apparently they had just sat in front of the TV after school.

Mrs. B. now feels that she can rely on the center and be free to progress in her own position, which will help her provide better for her children. She has sought and received advice from the director and in parent meetings organized through the center. This year she offered to take responsibility for being on the parent committee to plan such meetings and is enjoying the contact with other mothers who are also on their own.

What about Timothy?

Can Tim continue to feel good about himself and the program as the years go on and activities are changed and modified as his interests change?

And His Mother?

Will Mrs. B.'s participation in center activities enrich her own life?

After this experience, will she be a parent who participates in public school as well?

How can the center program maintain Mrs. B.'s interest in helping out and taking responsibility for the program for both children and parents?

Can the center continue to recruit young men students as assistants or volunteers to provide for the interests of children like Tim?

Daily Activities and Schedules

A good school-age child care center is a home away from home where children can play and learn. It is a safe place for parents to leave children, knowing they will be happy and well cared for. A good child care center is an extension of, not a substitute for, the home, so the center staff must see both parents and children as integral parts of the child care family.

A quality child care program is not a babysitting service but is planned by staff who know how children grow and develop. They are people who are interested in, and feel responsible for, seeing that the day-to-day experiences of the children take place in an environment which promotes growth and learning. Centers are usually staffed by people with special training, although some child care centers are organized and administered by parents.

A child care program for children five to ten years of age serves children before and after school hours and during lunch when there is no public school lunch program. It is also open from early morning to late afternoon during holiday and vacation periods.

The child care center staff, like the staff of any organization dealing with children, recognizes that it is an educational force. Each person on the staff serves as an example to the children, since children learn by observing as much as, if not more than, by

being "taught." Parents in the home teach in this same way.

ENCOURAGING PARENT INVOLVEMENT

It is important for staff to support the bond between parent and child by including parents as well as children in program planning, by inviting parents to participate in as many activities as their schedules allow, and by sharing their special knowledge of children in frequent and supportive conferences and group discussions.

Parents can learn in this nondirective way as they see staff handle problems similar to those they deal with at home. That is why it is important for centers to be open to parents and for parents and child care personnel to become mutually supportive, both enriching and enhancing the quality of life for the children.

Brief meetings can be held with parents as they drop off their children, bring discarded materials from their jobs or from home for center projects, contribute ideas on community trips or activities to be shared with other parents, and give brief but helpful reports on the child's evening or weekends at home. If parents feel a part of the program, they

are more likely to volunteer, attend parent meetings, join parent trips, and participate in other spontaneous ways.

A TYPICAL DAY

Transitions

Even for school-age children the times of transition from one setting to another can be difficult. Sometimes, in the morning, children may need to sit close to the teacher and absorb a little tender loving care to help them through the school day. Similar relaxing times may be needed on their return from school.

During the school year the children spend one to three hours in the center before going to school (see Fig. 1). This is the time for finishing homework, possibly with the help of a staff member; relaxing after a hurried breakfast at home; cleaning up and getting ready for school; or playing quiet indoor games.

Learning to live together takes time. All groups of children will have problems, but an understanding adult can encourage everyone to learn to talk things through and get the other person's point of view when children are unable to resolve their own conflicts.

Coordinating Different Schedules

Naturally there are times of the day when, because of the nature of the activity or because older children are away at school, children may be grouped together in age-similar groups. However, during the hours when the whole age span from preschool toddlers to older school-age children are present, age groupings should be flexible, depending on the activity. Sometimes older children will help younger children; sometimes they will all participate in an activity.

Special Planning

During vacation and holiday periods (see Fig. 2) when the children are in the center all day, special planning is necessary to ensure a wide variety of activities available for all children.

ENRICHING THE CENTER AND THE FAMILY

In the chapters which follow, suggestions for a variety of different activities have been developed. These can serve as guidelines for planning stimulating and meaningful programs with children for short or extended center hours. Lists of equipment, suggestions for storage, and a bibliography of additional readings are also included.

As you work with these materials, think about the many ways in which children learn. Think also about your role as parent educator, remembering always that parent education works best if it is done in a supportive, empathetic environment rather than in a judgmental, didactic one. Many smaller nuclear families who use child care facilities lead relatively isolated lives with little opportunity to meet other families. Child care centers can serve families as community centers, in a sense replacing the extended family. Groups of parents from centers can often babysit for one another; spend holidays together; plan recreation projects; organize consumer cooperatives, special interest groups, and rap sessions; and participate in a multitude of other joint projects. This kind of cooperative endeavor will happen only if staff members facilitate parent involvement and extend caring, receptive attitudes to parents as well as children.

In addition to enriching family life, such cooperative efforts by families can also enrich the center, because parents who feel they are part of the center can serve very effectively as advocates, fundraisers, and contributors of materials and special skills.

For half-day kindergarten children the child care center is truly a home away from home. When some children attending the kindergarten program go home at noon, day care children go back to the center for a relaxed play and cleanup time before eating a good, hot lunch. After lunch and storytime, they settle down for the same afternoon rest that their schoolmates are having at home.

When the primary children (first and second graders) come back to the center at 2:00 p.m., the kindergarten children join them in a snack. Then all the children have an afternoon of self-selected activities with staff available as needed. There are many things for them to do and an informal atmosphere in which to do it. Much planning by the children and the staff goes into setting up the ever-changing environment.

Indoor activities such as arts and crafts, music and dancing, puzzles and card games, books and records help children learn about numbers, discover new words, and explore science concepts. These activities sharpen children's abilities to listen and observe; they are vital for children who are learning to read.

Outdoors there is jumping rope and roller skating, climbing on the jungle gym and the rings—activities which help children feel comfortable with their bodies. Mastery of such skills helps growing children feel capable and confident.

At 3:00 p.m. the older children come back to the center. First there is a snack and planning time. Then a group of children may accompany younger children to a nearby park for various activities, walk to the public library for books, or go to the store to buy the model kit for which they have been saving. They often need to run and climb, kick balls, and pound punching bags; they enjoy organizing competitive games. Other children may prefer to engage in art, music, or construction projects, or to complete homework. Sometimes, especially toward late afternoon, there is a quiet game around the table—Monopoly, bingo, hearts, Sorry! or lotto. Occasionally there is a special television show suitable for children of various ages. Although aimless television viewing is discouraged, there are times when this medium enhances developing knowledge and skills. Staff should be alert for this kind of program and include it as a center activity.

Eight-, nine-, and ten-year-old children need a trusted adult close by, an adult who stays in the background but is available when needed. Children of this age are individualists who should be allowed freedom to engage in self-directed activities as long as they do not disrupt other children.

Each day during the year there are housekeeping chores which are done cooperatively by all the children. The center is truly a children's center, so everyone helps to clean up and keep things in order, making the center a homelike place.

Figure 1

School Year—Suggested Schedule

7:00-9:30 a.m.	**Center opens.** Arrival of children in accordance with parents' scheduled work hours and children's school hours. Breakfast. Morning program adapted to interests, age levels, and hours of attendance in regular school classes. **Indoor activities** such as construction projects with blocks and accessory materials; language and literature activities with books, stories, discussion, conversation; materials such as puzzles, scissors, pegboards; card games; study area for children who want to finish their homework; records for listening; cooking.
12:00 noon	**Lunch** in school cafeteria or at the center for kindergarten children.
12:30-3:00 p.m.	**Kindergarten children:** Rest-washing-snack-indoor activities. Opportunities which help meet physical needs, establish routine habits, and foster positive health attitudes.
2:00 p.m.	**Grades 1 and 2:** Snack, choice of indoor or outdoor activities (see 3-5 p.m. activities).
3:00 p.m.	**Grades 3, 4, and 5:** Snack, choice of indoor or outdoor activities (see 3-5 p.m. activities).
3:00-5:00 p.m.	**Indoor activities:** Blocks and accessory materials; puppets and housekeeping play; puzzles and card games; music and art materials; reading; sewing, craft projects, and hobbies; study; creative dramatics; creative writing; office assistance; science and nature projects.
	Outdoor activities: Physical activities which involve running, hopping, skipping, jumping, balancing, climbing; team sports and organized games; dramatic play with boxes, ladders, boards, tarps, barrels, blocks, and other materials; gardening; woodworking; craft projects and hobbies; science and nature projects; mud, sand, and water play; walks in the neighborhood; trips to nearby places of interest. Children released for Scouts, Camp Fire Girls, Boys Club, Girls Club, YMCA, YWCA, swimming, recreation centers, dance lessons, music lessons, upon receipt of written permission from parents.
5:00-6:00 p.m.	**Inside and outside cleanup.** Preparation for going home. Individual and small group indoor activities. Center closes.

Figure 2

Vacations and Holidays—Suggested Schedule

7:00-9:30 a.m.	**Center opens.** Arrival of children in accordance with parents' scheduled work hours. Breakfast. Morning program adapted to interests, age levels, and hours of attendance. **Indoor activities** with blocks and similar materials; materials such as puzzles, scissors, pegboards; card games; records for listening; sewing, library corner; cooking.
9:30-11:30 a.m.	**Snacktime.** Children help prepare and assist with snack, serving, and cleanup. Indoor and outdoor activities, group and individual, such as puppetry, woodworking, housekeeping play, music and body movement, handicrafts, cooking and baking, gardening, walks, trips, swimming at the Y or community or school pools, outdoor games, soccer, day camping, play on outdoor climbing equipment, creative writing, drama, art, carpentry, mechanics, block building construction activities, picnics, tetherball, roller skating, cycling, ping-pong, shuffleboard.
11:30 a.m.-2:00 p.m.	**Routine activities.** Washing up for lunch. Lunch. Children assist with preparation, setting tables, serving, and cleanup. **Rest time** according to age and needs of the children. **Quiet activities** such as reading, listening to records, card games, puzzles, dominoes, checkers, chess, sewing, knitting, art activities, creative writing.
2:00-5:00 p.m.	**Afternoon snack.** Children help prepare and assist with serving and cleanup. **Indoor and outdoor activities,** group and individual, should vary from those used in the morning (see 9:30-11:30 a.m.). Children released for Scouts, Camp Fire Girls, Boys Club, Girls Club, YMCA, YWCA, swimming, recreation centers, dance lessons, music lessons, upon receipt of written permission from parents.
5:00-6:00 p.m.	**Inside and outside cleanup.** Preparation for going home. Individual and small group indoor activities. Center closes.

Routines: Ruts or Routes to Learning?

2

The daily routines of coming and going, mealtimes and snacktimes, rest, grooming, and cleanup make up the basic framework of the program in an all-day child care center. These activities are often dull and monotonous, but they need not be if a family atmosphere of helpfulness and cooperation is established.

How can this be done? First of all, it is important to find out how staff members feel about daily routines. Are they a bore? Are they chores to be completed somehow in order to get on with more important activities? Are they jobs that have to be done in a certain way, day in and day out? Or are they activities which are never done the same way twice? How can they be capitalized upon to promote children's growth and development?

When you think of the number of hours children spend every day washing, eating, resting, and cleaning up after themselves, you realize how important it is for children to enjoy routines, to learn from them and accept them as part of their everyday living. The pace for handling routines may have to be slower, with time taken to encourage children in their first efforts at sweeping, pie cutting, or dishwashing. It may be necessary to become a little less or more organized than one usually is. However, it will be worth the effort if the children begin to feel that the necessary routines of life can be as interesting as other parts of the day.

ARRIVALS AND DEPARTURES

Hellos and goodbyes are so important. Parents as well as children need the security of knowing that someone at the center knows the child has arrived or is leaving. Greetings and goodbyes act as bridges. They help children cross over safely from home to center to school and back again. If a health check is included as part of the greeting, be sure the children know that you are interested in them, not just in their runny noses. Be sure to call children by name so that they know you know them; find out the name each child wants you to use.

The *way* you say "hello" or "goodbye" is even more important. Children can tell from your expression and tone of voice whether they are really welcome and whether you are sorry or glad to see them go. Arrivals and departures can be times for shared confidences—lunch box contents, dreams, TV shows, birthday presents, plans for the evening. Learn to listen to what the children are saying.

Hellos and goodbyes form the vital link between home, center, and school. They provide a chance to exchange brief reports about what the child is doing, to set dates for parent conferences, and, most of all, to let parents know you care about them and their children.

Learning to live together takes time. All groups of children will have problems, but an understanding adult can encourage everyone to learn to talk things through and get the other person's point of view.

MEALTIMES AND SNACKTIMES

We can all have fun preparing and eating food together. Mealtimes in an all-day program can provide a sense of family that is so important in the lives of children. Pleasant mealtime conversations bring children and staff members in closer touch with each other; they feed children emotionally as well as physically. Mealtimes often become a time for sharing triumphs and tragedies, providing the setting for humorous or serious discussions. Children who help set the table, prepare and serve food, and clean up gain a feeling of confidence and importance in contributing to the group.

Mealtime routines can be varied frequently although family-style meals with serving dishes at the table will probably be the choice most of the time. But what could be more fun than a picnic lunch on the playground, a chance for the builders to eat lunch in the block fortress they made, or breakfast in the playhouse with a best friend? Holidays and birthdays may call for special kinds of meals; children will eagerly join in the festive spirit of such occasions. For all meals, children can make the table setting attractive, help with food preparation, and have the chance to serve others, too.

Snacktimes should also be varied. Sometimes children will sit down together for a snack; at other times, children will be so involved in what they are doing that snacks can be left out on a table or "snack stand" for children to enjoy when they have time.

The chance to try a variety of foods will encourage many children to eat new things. If mealtimes are relaxed, with emphasis on consideration for others rather than formal manners, children will begin to develop good eating habits and good manners as well. Both snacks and meals can be planned with children to ensure a balanced and interesting diet. Favorite recipes can be shared with parents, who may wish to share their favorites with the center (see Chapter 12 on cooking).

REST

The amount of rest children need will vary according to age, temperament, types of activity, weather, and energy level. Rest periods can be pleasurable —a time to sit and look at a book, to play a quiet game, to cozy into a corner with a blanket and pillow. Younger children may still want and need to sleep in a separate area; older children may enjoy resting through a low-key activity such as sewing, checkers, or reading.

A relaxed atmosphere and attitude on the part of the staff will set the stage for a relaxing rest period.

Mealtimes and snacks can provide a sense of family that is so important in the lives of children.

Some centers have found that a brief selection of soft background music will help some children relax. Some staff members may read to a small group of children; others may go with a few children to a corner of the room for a quiet table game or a discussion. Rest period should not be so long that it becomes a battleground between staff and children. What many children need are frequent, relatively short periods of quiet time during the day.

CLEANUP

Children should help the staff plan for cleanup following all activities and check their own progress in carrying out their responsibilities.

Sharing in cleanup jobs helps children develop a feeling of partnership with other children and the staff. Children develop a sense of pride in their part in making the center look attractive and neat.

Sometimes a child will not feel like helping or will be overwhelmed by an assigned task. Staff members can be of special help at such times, working along with the child, allowing for flexibility, and giving well-deserved recognition to the child who follows through on a difficult or disliked task. Emphasize cooperation rather than competition—except for the child's own attempts to do better each time.

GROOMING AND PERSONAL HABITS

The center can encourage good grooming and personal habits in many ways. Each child should have a special place to store an individually marked brush, comb, toothbrush, and any other personal items. Mirrors and facilities at child-height in the bathroom will encourage attention to personal habits. While restroom facilities should always be available for children's use, additional time can be set aside before meals and after rest periods for handwashing, hair brushing, and general grooming.

The center staff can encourage a greater interest in good grooming by keeping on hand a supply of hand lotion, talcum powder, good smelling soap, ribbons for hairbows, shoe polish, needles and thread. An adult giving a helping hand with a new hairdo or a compliment on a good job of hand scrubbing will encourage children to make the effort to look their best. When they work with food, children will also have a chance to learn important health rules about clean hands and nails, etc.

TIPS FOR HANDLING ROUTINES

In planning for routines, here are some important points to remember:

1. Don't rush yourself or the children. Use the time spent in the activity to get to know the children better and use the learning opportunities available.

2. Enjoy the activity for its own sake. Plan the activity so that you and the children will not only have a sense of satisfaction when it is done but a sense of enjoyment while doing it.

3. Let the children do as much as possible themselves. Children can assist in planning for routines. Provide equipment which children can manage. If necessary, explain what needs to be done, then stand by to help and encourage them.

4. Vary routines as you would any other activity. Routines are the stable framework of each day, but they need not be repetitive.

5. Remember that children are learning all the time and routine times are no exception. Mathematics is used in setting tables; language skills are involved in reading and following directions; opportunities for developing good health habits come at mealtimes, rest, grooming, and cleanup times. In addition, routine activities make it possible for children to grow in self-reliance, responsibility, and cooperation.

A good physical development program provides children with endless opportunities for calculated risk-taking, creating self-challenging activities, and predicting and measuring successes.

Active Play: Moving to Learn

3

Leaping, striding, climbing, twisting, and running! What better way to experience exhilaration and sheer joy than through the mastery of one's own body! A good physical development program provides children with endless opportunities for calculated risk-taking, creating self-challenging activities, and predicting and measuring successes.

Active play in a balanced school-age program can and should include many facets. Included in such a program should be organized games where children can experience forming and working together in teams, making and following rules, and problem solving. Self-challenging activities, in which the children set goals for and compete against themselves, are especially important. Activities such as gymnastics, calisthenics, and track and field activities should be included regularly. Skills acquisition activities also play a part in a good program; children should be provided with the chance to climb, jump, balance, swing, run, twist, and tumble, either through organized activities or through activities they have initiated and chosen themselves. Learning to make the large muscles in the body perform on command, mastering new skills, and positioning the body in space are all necessary vehicles for feelings of success and competence in every child.

Active play should also mean that children are provided with the opportunity to participate in creative movement, music, and dance. And most important, children must be allowed the opportunity to create and involve themselves in open-ended, child-centered active play in which the adult plays no specific part, and which allows the children time to run, leap, invent characters, set situations, shout, and just *be*.

Through successful participation in physical activities, children—

- develop a feeling of self-worth,

- develop courage and self-confidence to try increasingly more difficult tasks such as climbing higher and exploring new ways to perform skills,

- practice self-reliance and self-expression through creative activities such as music and dance,

- grow in ability to exercise fair play,

- have opportunities to be of service as leaders and followers through participating in games and other activities.

Wanting to touch things is perfectly natural! How much children can learn through their skin and nerves—hot and cold, soft and hard, smooth and rough. Muscles are also a source of learning —light and heavy, strong and weak.

Active physical movement is imperative for both children and adults to remain in good health. The lymph, blood, and other systems of the body function best with periods of activity ranging from exertion to rest.

Learning to move freely and joyously is an essential part of growing up, and older children may wish to work with and encourage younger children to develop new skills as they express interest.

Movement is made up of elements of time, space, and force which coordinate into an act of moving. In movement through space, children learn direction (forward, backward, sideways, diagonally); level (high, low); size (small, large; wide, narrow); force (light, heavy; quiet, noisy); and time (fast, slow; even, uneven).

Essential to the success of the entire program is ample, well-designed space which is adaptable to a number of uses. Both indoor and outdoor areas should be available for vigorous and creative movement activities. Care should be exercised in planning to ensure that sound levels will not interfere with other simultaneous activities of groups or individuals. Quiet space, after a busy school day, can be just as important as opportunities for expression through loud voices.

Storage space for the equipment and materials which can enhance children's play must also be well-planned for maximum organization and protection from vandalism. Staff and children can share in the care and proper storage of these valuable additions to the program.

Safety should remain a primary consideration both indoors and out. Staff should be well-versed in first aid procedures, and first aid kits should be placed in several readily accessible areas. Local licensing regulations usually set minimum standards. Also check on insurance policies which may be necessary to protect both staff and children.

Permanent Equipment

Balance beam—metal or wooden, adjustable
Bars—horizontal and parallel, low for turning
Basketball goals—lower than standard
Blocks—hollow *(see Chapter 5)*
Cargo net
Cement pipes for crawling through
Climbing apparatus
Climbing pole(s)—like tetherball or higher
   poles
Ladder—horizontal
Mats—5' × 10' minimum, for tumbling
Piano and other musical instruments
Poles or logs embedded in earth
Record player and records
Rings—safely mounted at various heights
Ropes—two, about two feet apart, for swing-
   ing between trees
Sandbox
Tetherball equipment
Tires—for climbing through or as swings
Walls for hitting balls against

Active physical movement is imperative for both children and adults to remain in good health.

Specially Marked Areas

Squares for four-square game
Number and letter squares
Hopscotch
Shuffleboard

Learning Materials

Ballons
Balls—soft plastic fleece balls; crocheted balls
    stuffed with old stockings; rubber balls, 6",
    8", 13"; utility ball, 8½"; softball; and basket-
    ball
Barrel—55 gallon steel drum to crawl through
Bats—unbreakable plastic and/or wood
Beanbags
Cones—for hurdles or goals
Frisbees
Hoops—can be made from ½" polytheline
    hose or ⅝" doweling, glue, and electri-
    cian's tape
Inner tube—cut in pieces for pulling
Inner tubes—inflated
Jump rope—#12 sash cord, nylon or plastic
Jumping boards
Mirror
Nets
Paddles—wooden or made from metal
    clotheshanger covered with silk or nylon
Parachute—16', from surplus stores
Pump—for air for balls
Rings—deck tennis (rubber)
Sawhorses
Scarves and props for dancing
Stilts—made with cord and cans or purchased
    wood or aluminum
Stopwatch
Wands—36" batons or dowels
Yo-yos

Storage

Bicycle racks
Dowel pegs or hooks—for hanging hoops,
    jump ropes
Padlock and chain—for securing items such
    as tires to fence
Pegboard—attached to wall, marked for hang-
    ing small items
Sandbox cover
Shelves

TOPICS TO TALK ABOUT WITH CHILDREN

Care and storage of equipment.

Forming of teams—assessing strengths and weak-
nesses.

Individual assessment—methods for measuring
individual progress in skill-building activities.

Different methods of building particular skills.

Combining skills and materials for creative dance.

Developing awareness of movement and growth.

Need for consistent rules for participation in organized activities.

Safety in using special equipment.

Roles of supervisory adults.

IDEAS TO TRY

Arrange tournaments or decathalons for mastering
particular skills.

Children can prepare individualized charts to measure their progress in certain activities.

Children can use a stopwatch to measure and
record their progress in self-challenging activities.
Stress that children are only in competition with
themselves.

Form teams and elect team captains for sports such
as softball (or tee-ball for younger children),
volleyball, badminton, and soccer.

Children can create an obstacle course using barrels, tires, inner tubes, tumbling mats, and other
equipment.

Children can invent relay games.

Creative movement activities can involve props
(scarves, capes, hats, umbrellas, crepe paper)
and music selected by the participants.

Study different ethnic folk dances; design and
make authentic apparel.

Arrange for "activity days" (bike day, skating day,
gymnastics day) when children bring their equipment from home.

Plan a "Junior Olympics" activity involving children from a neighboring school or center.

Maintain an equipment storage area available on a
daily basis for children's selections.

Encourage the use of special accessories to enhance
movement experiences (balloons for balancing
games and relays, blindfolds for sensory experiences, etc.).

Children can create their own climbing and/or
balancing structures by collecting plastic milk
storage boxes.

Create an interest center within the classroom
using exercise ropes, tumbling mat, beanbag
toss, etc.

A record player, an assortment of records, and
instruments can be available at all times for
spontaneous music or dance activities—ask
children to bring their favorite records.

GAMES

Lemonade: Two teams. Each team decides on a trade, such as "plumber." Members of one team walk up to the other and say, "Here we come." Other team asks, "Where from?" First team: (name of town). Second team: "What's your trade?" First team: "Lemonade." Second team: "Give us some." First team pantomimes plumbing using plunger, wrench, twisting pipe, etc. As soon as the second team guesses the trade, they shout the answer and chase the players on the first team back to their baseline, catching as many as possible. The ones who are caught join their captors and the second team chooses a trade and the game is repeated.

Run, Sheep, Run: Two groups of players each select a leader. One group goes out to hide as a unit. The leader of that group returns to the goal and indicates that her group is ready to be found. She warns her group through a code of signals which mean to stand still, lie low, move toward the goal, etc. If any member of the group searching sees one of the hidden group, she notifies her leader who at once calls, "Run, sheep, run." All the players then run as quickly as possible to the goal. The group arriving at the goal first goes out to hide.

Breaking the Line: Children stand in a circle and hold hands with the children on either side. Choose one child—"It"—to stand in the center of the circle. "It" tries to break out of the circle by separating the hands of the children. If he escapes from the circle, the children chase him. The first one to catch him becomes "It."

What Did I Do? Children stand facing one direction. One child goes behind the children and jumps, skips, hops, claps, etc., and then asks, "What did I do?" Child who guesses first has the next turn to be the leader.

I Spy: A child hides an object and the other children try to find it. The leader claps or beats a drum loudly when they are close and softly when they are far from the object.

Wiggle Waggle: A child is chosen to be "It." She names different parts of the body, such as nose, head, right ear, left hand, right foot, left leg. As she names the part, the children wiggle the part named.

Relays: All kinds. One that children like is Over and Under. Have two or three teams. Give the first player of each team a ball, a beanbag, or some other object. At a signal the leader passes the object over her head to the second player who in turn passes it between his knees to the third person who passes it over her head to the fourth person, and so on. When it reaches the last person, he runs to the head of the line and starts the object back once again. The game continues until everyone on the team has regained his or her original position, with the first player back at the head of the line. The line finishing first wins the race.

Other games: Follow the Leader, Hare and Hounds, Prisoners' Base, Squirrels in Trees, Going to Jerusalem, Fruit Basket, Numbers, Restaurant, Fox and Hen, Circle, Tag, Hopscotch.

Resources

Arnold, A. *The World Book of Children's Games.* New York: Fawcett World Publishing, 1975.

Barlin, A., and Barlin, P. *The Art of Learning Through Movement.* Los Angeles: Ward Ritchie Press, 1971.

Bartal, L., and Ne'eman, V. *Movement Awareness and Creativity.* New York: Harper & Row, 1975.

Blitner, J. *Hop, Skip, Jump, Read.* Long Beach, Calif.: Christian Press, 1972.

Burton, E.C. *The New Physical Education for Elementary School Children.* Boston: Houghton Mifflin, 1976.

Cherry, C. *Creative Play for the Developing Child.* Belmont, Calif.: Fearon, 1976.

Clark, C. *Evaluating Motor Development of the Young Child.* Los Angeles County Superintendent of Schools, 9300 E. Imperial Highway, Downey, Calif. 90242, 1966.

Corbin, C.B. *Inexpensive Equipment for Games, Play, and Physical Activities.* Dubuque, Iowa: William C. Brown, 1972.

Cratty, B.J., et al. *Movement Activities, Motor Ability and the Education of Children.* Springfield, Ill.: Charles C. Thomas, 1970.

Engstrom, G., ed. *The Significance of the Young Child's Motor Development.* Washington, D.C.: National Association for the Education of Young Children, 1971.

Hellison, D.R. *Humanistic Physical Education.* Englewood Cliffs, N.J.: Prentice-Hall, 1973.

Hendricks, C.G., and Wills, R. *The Centering Book: Awareness Activities for Children, Parents and Teachers.* Englewood Cliffs, N.J.: Prentice-Hall, 1975.

Housing for Early Childhood Education—Centers for Growing and Learning. Washington, D.C.: Association for Childhood Education International, 1968.

International Council on Health, Physical Education, and Recreation. *ICHPER Book of Worldwide Games and Dances.* Washington, D.C.: American Association for Health, Physical Education, and Recreation, 1967.

Jameson, K., and Kidd, P. *Pre-School Play.* Cincinnati, Ohio: Van Nostrand Reinhold, 1974.

Kritchevsky, W.W. *Practical Application of the Expressive Arts in Elementary Education.* Pasadena, Calif.: Pacific Oaks, 1973.

Laban, R. *The Mastery of Movement*. rev. ed. Boston: Plays, 1971.

Millen, N. *Children's Games from Many Lands*. New York: Friendship Press, 1965.

North, M. *Movement Education: Child Development Through Body Motion*. New York: E.P. Dutton, 1973.

Physical Education for Children's Healthful Living. Washington, D.C.: Association for Childhood Education International, 1968.

"Playscapes." Washington, D.C.: Association for Childhood Education International, 1973.

Schurr, E. L. *Movement Experiences for Children: A Humanistic Approach to Elementary School Physical Education*. Englewood Cliffs, N.J.: Prentice-Hall, 1975.

Singer, R.N. *Motor Learning and Human Performance: An Application in Physical Education Skills*. New York: Macmillan, 1975.

Stone, J.G. *A Guide to Discipline*. Washington, D.C.: National Association for the Education of Young Children, 1969.

Taylor, J. *Dance/Movement Experiences*. Inglewood, Calif.: Educational Insights, 1974.

Werner, P.H., and Simmons, R.A. *Inexpensive Physical Equipment for Children*. Minneapolis, Minn.: Burgess, 1976.

Arts and Crafts
4

There are many reasons why art experiences are important learning experiences for children. Materials are so colorful and interesting. Children can cut, shape, glue, tie, arrange, and rearrange them according to individual wishes. Children can take their time, start over, be playful, experiment, manipulate, and help satisfy their endless curiosity: "What happens when I mix red with blue?" "Will this kind of glue stick to metal?"

Using real tools and materials, children can create things they feel proud of and which others will enjoy and admire. Children can work with art materials alone (even in a room full of other people), or they can enjoy the company of special friends. By capturing moments of their lives in a variety of shapes, forms, and colors, children can continue to enjoy these reminders of people they know and places they have been.

With art children can describe their feelings, experiences, wishes, and ideas in ways that have meaning for them and are understandable to others; for example, a sheet of paper covered with blazing red and orange that the child describes as "a fire," or a fancy, detailed farm scene with a horse and rider that says, "I wish I had a horse. If I did, it would look like this, and I would ride it." Through pounding clay, covering a sheet of paper with dark colors, or meaningless repetition of drawings, children can also express feelings—feelings they may not be able to express in words.

Painting or drawing with bright or gloomy colors, slicking and smoothing a clay fish with water, using soft cotton for clouds, making rough scratchy lines with an almost dry brush, children can learn how color, shape, size, and texture make the finished product look the way it does. As they choose and combine objects of different colors, shapes, and textures, children learn to become more careful observers of the materials they are using and of the world around them.

Arts and crafts projects can teach children new ways of creating with ordinary things: making mobiles and wire sculptures from coathangers; using clay for beads, pendants, and plaques, as well as for bowls and figures; painting on cardboard, wood, and foil, as well as paper. Such projects can stimulate children to think up their own ways of using almost anything to create something new.

Cutting and twisting wires, rolling clay, balancing the delicate parts of a mobile, lifting and carrying, all help children learn to work with their large and small muscles and develop hand-eye coordination. Opportunities to cut metal with tin snips, punch holes in leather with an awl, saw on a curved line with a coping saw, glaze and fire special clay products, take and develop photographs, help children learn to use a variety of tools and equipment skillfully and safely. Choosing a project, listening to or reading directions, planning, making a decision as to what tools and supplies to use, sticking with the project over a period of time, solving problems, working together or asking for help, all of these help children develop effective work habits. Children also learn that cleaning up and returning materials and equipment to their storage place is important if these things are to be found the next time they are needed.

Big projects such as painting and decorating a puppet stage or composing a mural, or small projects done at the same table or in the same area, can help children learn to work together—to take turns, share, give and accept help, and value and protect other children's work. Through such projects children have opportunities to find out that not everyone likes the same things and that this is all right.

Working together or alone, children hear and learn to use new words to describe their tools, materials, and processes involved in their projects. They have many opportunities to find out and talk about one another's plans, ideas, needs, and feelings. Reading directions and labels on supplies and shelves and using books about how our ancestors worked with arts and crafts help children enrich their vocabularies and understand how reading can be both useful and interesting.

Meaningful art experiences can promote a growing awareness of esthetics—developing an appreciation for beauty through balance, form, line, and color. Individuals can evaluate their skills and selection of materials as they mature in their understanding of the many facets of art exploration. Comparing and contrasting various cultural art forms and expressions can lead to new insights about the universality of expression through art.

Children can coordinate their experiences in a variety of other activities through art—writing and illustrating a book detailing the emergence of a butterfly or creating stage sets for an original musical production. Many projects can take on new dimensions when they are taken outdoors to a table or a grassy spot under a cool tree. Whatever its form, art can enhance children's understandings of themselves and the world around them.

20

Permanent Equipment

Air sprayer
Aprons
Brayer
Brushes—various sizes, types, and shapes
Camera
Clay boards
Crochet hooks
Dark room equipment
Drip cloths
Drying rack, shelves
Easels, bulletin boards, display screens
Hole punches
Linoleum tools and blocks
Looms
Matting knife
Modeling and stamping tools for leather
Mounting pins
Needles—knitting, sewing; varied sizes
Paper cutter
Plastic bottles, tubs
Rags and towels for cleanup
Rubber bands
Scissors—right- and left-handed styles
Sewing machine
Sponges
Stamp pads
Staplers

Learning Materials

Absorbent cotton
Beads, feathers, sequins
Cardboard—various weights and sizes
Chalk—assorted colors

Arts and crafts projects can teach children new ways of creating with ordinary things—using clay for beads.

Charcoal
Clay—commercial
Cloth—various widths, colors, textures designs
Copper
Cottage cheese cartons and lids
Crayons
Dyes of various colors, types
Enamel paints
Felt pens
Film
Finger paints
Foil, aluminum
Gummed tape—assorted widths
Liquid soap
Mesh screening
Metallic thread
Modeling media—flour and salt, plasticine, sawdust
Natural items—acorns, seeds, grasses, flowers, cones, stones, pebbles, corn shucks, leaves, nutshells
Paper—crepe, gummed, tissue, construction, butcher, parchment, easel, newsprint, white drawing, waxed, roll for murals, old telephone books, wallpaper books
Paper bags, plates, boxes, picture files
Paste, glue, rubber cement
Pencils
Pins
Pipe cleaners
Plaster of paris
Plastic paint
Potato mashers
Reed raffia
Ribbons, rickrack, edging
Sand
Shellac
Soap bars for sculpting
Soap flakes
Spools—wood and plastic

Starch
Styrofoam—various shapes and sizes
Tempera paints
Thread—sewing, embroidery
Tiles—wall board
Turpentine
Vegetable colors
Water colors
Water soluble inks
Wax
Wire
Wire coathangers
Yarns

Storage

Boxes, baskets, barrels, and shelves for organized storage

Labels for storage units—store items used together in one place

Shelves of different heights and widths

Racks or hooks for aprons—near area where they will be used

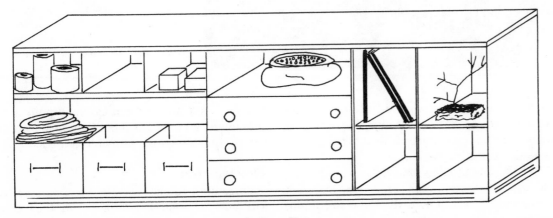

Storage Unit

TOPICS TO TALK ABOUT WITH CHILDREN

Care and safe use of tools, preparation of materials and equipment.

Steps to be considered and materials needed for projects—children may wish to list what they will be doing.

Materials can be brought from home—empty spools, egg cartons, plastic containers, etc.

Creative use of odds and ends for collages.

Children may want to plan for an art show of their projects—another center or school could be invited, as well as parents.

What happens to paint when water, starch, soap, or sand is added?

Discovering new ways to use familiar materials —tempera paint, finger paint, water paint, colors, charcoal, colored chalk, clay, dough clay, crayons, felt pens, soap.

Ways older children can work with younger children to complete a difficult project.

How to make mats and picture frames.

New words—*titanium white, ivory black, cadmium orange, cadmium yellowlight, thalocyamine blue, alizanin, crimson, yellow, ochre, burnt sienna.* New ideas for some children—hot and cold colors (red, orange, and yellow; blue, green, and purple); primary colors (red, yellow, and blue); secondary colors (mixtures of two primary colors—red, and yellow make orange; blue and yellow make green; blue and red make purple).

Children may wish to make plans for trips to art exhibits and museums. What arrangements need to be made?

Who might children know—a grandparent, neighbor, sister, or brother—who can teach children a new skill or technique or discuss art objects from another culture?

IDEAS TO TRY

Clay and other modeling media

Commercial clay (gray or terra-cotta). Wet commercial clay is easiest to use, although it is also available in powdered form. Wet clay must be kept in an airtight container, such as a plastic bag, with a wet sponge to keep it damp and ready for use.

String or wire can be used to cut lumps at least the size of a grapefruit for each child. A hard surface such as a board or linoleum block makes work with clay and cleanup easier. Any clay temporarily not being worked with should be covered with a damp cloth until the entire project is finished. Few tools are needed for work with clay—designs may be scratched in with fingernails or other objects; textured items can be added or used to vary the surface. Children may wish to explore several types of construction: slab, pinch, coiling, draping.

21

If a kiln is available for firing the clay, all air bubbles must be removed from the object. Check on details before undertaking projects of this magnitude.

Plasticine. Plasticine is readily available, but children may prefer more natural clays or modeling media which can be mixed easily and inexpensively in the classroom.

Dough clays. Several recipes are available for variety in texture, ease of storage, and possibilities for reuse. Experiment to find the children's favorite types.

Flour and salt clay

| 4 cups flour | Food coloring |
| 1 cup salt | Water to moisten |

Mix the ingredients to desired dampness. Store in refrigerator to avoid spoiling. This clay dries hard and can be painted or decorated with pens.

To make reusable dough, add two tablespoons of cooking oil.

Sawdust modeling

| 2 cups sawdust | 1 cup flour or wheat paste. |
| Liquid starch | 1 tablespoon glue (if flour is used) |

Mix to workable consistency. Can be dried and painted.

Collage

A base of a paper plate, shirt cardboard, construction paper, wood, wall board, boxes, or any surface which will hold a variety of materials can be used. Glue may be needed as a better adhesive than paste for heavier items. Children should be encouraged to consider size, shape, color, and variety. Lace, flowers, shells, velvet, netting, satin, styrofoam, pipe cleaners, paper lace doilies, pieces of cork, yarn, and buttons are just some of the materials that can be used. If at all possible, use nonfood items for all craft uses—other materials have more satisfactory qualities.

Wax collage is a variety children may wish to try if adequate safety precautions are taken. Materials and equipment you will need are: hot plate, double boiler, wax, collage materials, and cardboard. Melt

Working with clay helps children learn to use their large and small muscles and develop hand-eye coordination.

wax in pan. Children then carefully pour a small amount of wax on cardboard to create a design and decorate hot wax with collage materials.

Construction

Three-dimensional constructions can be made with one or many materials, and they can be representational or abstract. Constructions which

22

remain fixed are called stabiles; those which are made to move are called mobiles.

Children will need to consider how things will be attached so they will hold together in a three-dimensional design. Wood, tongue depressors, swab sticks, wire, coathangers, wood pieces, aluminum foil, thread, corrugated cardboard may be used. Many interesting arrangements can be made by using cellophane, thin colored plastics, jewelry, colored sticks, colored string, and yarn. Cardboard tubes, pipe cleaners, pieces of wood, small wooden dowels, construction paper, and cardboard cylinders can be used for wood gluing.

Essential tools needed are scissors, cutting pliers, hammer, hole punch, and stapler. Thread, wire, string, yarn, or fine chain can be used for hanging mobiles, but bases are needed for stabiles. Stabiles and mobiles provide wonderful opportunities for creative expression—line, form, shapes, colors, textures, balance, and manipulation.

Cans and frozen food trays may be cut open, fringed, or the edges twisted with pliers. Holes punched in the pieces make them suitable for mobiles.

Toothpick, tongue depressor, straw, or string constructions can be made with paste or glue, scissors, and tissue paper. Toothpicks may be glued to a bent reed, pushed into a styrofoam base, or glued on wire. String constructions may be made on a notched cardboard or wood base with tubes and small boxes.

Toothpick Sculpture

Wire sculpture can be created from wire bent to form shapes and designs, curled around pencils, tubes, spools, or boxes. Stovepipe wire will retain shape. Scissors and pliers are needed. Mount on base if desired.

A footstool can be made from a box resting on four small blocks and glued into place. A pillow or pad is made to fit on the box. Top cover can be oilcloth or windowshade material for washability.

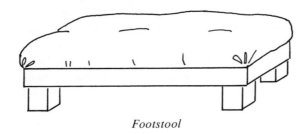

Footstool

Bookends can be made from small boxes which are decorated and then filled with sand.

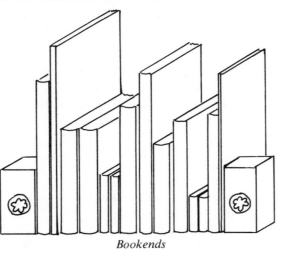

Bookends

Broom handles cut in thin slices make excellent **checkers** when painted red and black.

A delightful **wall hanging** can be made quickly from cloth such as felt or burlap, crayons, doweling, string, blunt needle for tapestry work, yarn or embroidery thread. Designs with crayons can be ironed with two pieces of paper folded around the fabric to absorb the wax. Yarn or thread can be used to sew the heading before inserting the dowel; the string is used for hanging the tapestry.

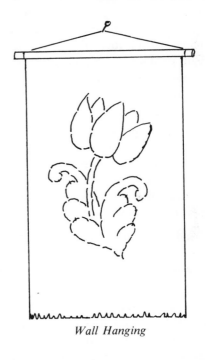

Wall Hanging

Aluminum foil will twist, bend, and squeeze into various shapes and designs. Fast drying cement may be used to join pieces together only when children are old enough to understand the extreme care needed to use the glue. Embellishments may be old jewelry, feathers, beads, enamel paints, ribbons.

Decorate jewelry boxes, wastepaper baskets, desk blotter sets, instruments, tote bags, knitting and sewing boxes.

Make animals, people, hats, transportation toys, miniature doll furniture, houses, pet cages, trays, sorting boxes, puppet theaters, shoeshine kits.

Crayons, colored chalk, charcoal, inks, felt pens, and pencils

Crayons can be used on the side if the paper covering is removed. Colors will be bright if there is a cushion of newspapers or magazines under the drawing paper. A pleated fold of construction paper or light cardboard makes a good holder for crayons, chalk, and charcoal.

Use pieces of torn cardboard or paper as a **stencil**—rub colored chalk or crayons along the edges of the stencil, put it on the paper and then brush the chalk off the stencil onto the paper with tissue. A pencil eraser can be used to rub the crayon onto the paper if a hard wax crayon is used. Nonaerosol hair spray or fixative should be used over chalk or charcoal work.

Crayon rubbings can be done on any thin paper over stones, leaves, cardboard pieces of various thicknesses and shapes, sandpaper, or corrugated paper.

To make a **crayon resist or etching,** cover white paper with crayons (use one or more crayons), then, using a black crayon, cover the entire paper. Use a blunt needle, nail, edge of scissors, or comb and scratch until design and colors show through. Thin paint (with a little liquid soap added) can also be used to cover the design.

Chalk painting can be done with the addition of starch on any kind of wet paper or cardboard. The end of the piece of chalk can be sharpened for fine work or blunted for thick lines. Use a tissue, rag, or fingers to mute and brush the colors.

Colored chalk soaked in a strong sugar-water solution for ten minutes will smear less while in use. A fixative for spraying colored chalk art work may be made by dissolving gum arabic in water until it is the consistency of cream. Use an empty spray bottle as container and spray.

Charcoal work can be done the same as chalk painting.

Melted crayons are a good way to use up small pieces. Cut or scrape pieces of crayon onto shiny shelf paper or finger paint paper and put this between two pieces of waxed paper. Cover with newspaper and press with warm iron to melt and spread the crayons.

For a variation, use two pieces of paper. Remove the top one after melting the crayons and scratch a design into the soft wax. Children can also put crayon pieces into bags and smash with a mallet. Bits of crayon are then sprinkled on paper and set out in the hot sun to melt.

Inks may be used on wet paper, as water colors or finger paints. Inks can also be used over crayon work.

Felt pens can be used singly or in combination with many other arts and crafts activities.

Pencils, lead of varied colors and degrees of hardness and softness, are vital for drawing activities. They can be combined with other media or used with graph paper for sketching and planning.

Scribble-Scrabbles

Construction paper
Pencils with thick, dark lead
Felt pens, crayons, waterproof ink and pen, or
   tempera paint and brush

Scribble design over entire paper in one continuous and abstract line. Outline portions of the pattern or design with felt pen, ink, or paint.

Old Masters Printing

Typing paper, white or colors—2 pieces	Wax crayons
Piece of window screen the size of the paper	Cloth or paper towels
Can of turpentine or mineral spirits	Cardboard or newspapers

Cover table with cardboard or newspapers. Draw design on paper placed over the screen, pressing heavily with the crayons. Lift picture off and spread back of paper with a thin coat of turpentine or mineral spirits; this will soften the wax crayon. Place another piece of paper over the drawing and rub with fingers until the picture is transferred as a monoprint. It may be possible to take two or three monoprints from the same drawing, as in finger painting.

Finger Painting

Finger painting can be done indoors or out on a variety of surfaces and in a number of ways. Experiment with different techniques and recipes. A few drops of oil of clove prevents distressing odors. Be sure to keep mixtures in covered jars in a cool location.

Finger Paint Mixture #1

1 cup liquid starch	6 cups warm water
½ cup soap chips	Dry tempera or food coloring

Dissolve soap chips with enough water and stir until all lumps have disappeared. Add to starch and remaining water. Keep in covered plastic jar until ready to use. Color may be added as children paint or in the mix.

Finger Paint Mixture #2

½ cup cornstarch

1⅓ cups boiling water

½ cup soap flakes

2 teaspoons glycerine

Dry tempera or food coloring

Dissolve cornstarch in boiling water until it is a cold cream consistency. Add soap flakes and glycerine and keep in covered jar. Color may be added to the mixture at this time or as the children paint.

Finger Paint Mixture #3

1½ cups laundry starch

1½ cups soap flakes

½ cup talcum powder (optional)

1 quart boiling water

Tempera paint (dry or liquid

Dissolve starch with some cold water until it is a cold cream consistency. Add the boiling water and cook until the finger paint mixture looks somewhat transparent. Keep stirring and add the talcum powder. Cook before adding the soap flakes, stirring until they are evenly distributed. Store in covered jars. Color may be added before placing in jar or when children are ready for work.

Finger Paint Mixture #4

Liquid starch

½ cup soap chips (optional)

Dry tempera or food coloring

Leave bottle of starch open for two or three days for the mixture to thicken, or add ½ cup of soap chips. Add color when ready to use finger paint.

Finger Paint Mixture #5

1 cup cornstarch

2 cups cold water

2 envelopes plain unflavored gelatin

4 cups boiling water

1 cup soap flakes

Dry tempera

Dissolve cornstarch in 1½ cups of cold water. Soak gelatin in remaining ½ cup of cold water. Add starch mixture to hot water slowly. Cook over medium heat, stirring constantly until mixture is thick and glossy. Blend in gelatin and soap flakes until dissolved. Divide into portions as desired and add tempera. Keep in covered jar.

Finger Paint Mixture #6

Wallpaper paste (wheat paste)

Tempera paint

Lukewarm water

Mix wallpaper paste into lukewarm water and stir until smooth. Add tempera paint. Measure your first try of this recipe and add either paste or water until you have the consistency you wish, then write the recipe for your file.

Monoprint from Finger Painting

Finger paint

Oilcloth taped to table or formica-covered tabletop

Waxed shelf paper or finger paint paper

Finger paint directly on the oilcloth or table surface. Press the waxed shelf paper or finger paint paper on top of the wet painting and smooth over entire surface with palm of hand until the painting is transferred to the paper. It may be possible to take two or three prints from the same finger painting. When dry, place painting face down between two pieces of newspaper and iron.

Jewelry

Beads from flour and salt

2 cups flour

2 cups salt

2 tablespoons powdered alum

Dry tempera or food coloring

Water

Toothpicks or nails

Rolling pin

String, narrow strips of leather, yarn, ribbon, or plastic lacing

Large ball of clay

Shellac

Brush (narrow bristles)

Alcohol for cleaning brush

Mix alum, flour, salt, water, and coloring until consistency of putty. It is now ready to be made into beads in a variety of ways:

- Make long coil and cut into pieces.
- Roll a piece between palms.
- Flatten out with rolling pin as if making dough ready for cookie cutter.

Using either a toothpick or nail, punch hole through each of the beads. Insert the toothpick or nail into hole and stick it into clay ball. Turn the nail or toothpick around in the beads from time to time to keep them from drying in the bead. Shellac beads when dry and then dry again.

Sizes and shapes may be irregular, and small beads can be placed between larger beads for design purposes. String may also be knotted between beads.

Leather

Leather scraps and pieces can be purchased. Needed are modeling and stamping tools, hole puncher, lacing, scissors, and a wooden mallet. Leather can be used on collages, glued onto wood as bookends, and made into billfolds, key rings, and other objects. Wet leather with sponge and press down with the modeler to bring desired design into relief.

Nature Crafts*

When working with natural objects, make certain conservation measures are followed to preserve living plants and animals.

You may wish to press and make leaf prints through spatter painting. Seeds can be used to make natural dyes and paints. Driftwood can serve as the base for stabiles.

Painting

Easel paint with tempera paints on cardboard, cloth, wood, construction paper. Paint indoors or out at tables, on floor, on boards attached to fences.

Spray paint (nonaerosol) boxes, boards, carpentry pieces, clay beads, pine cones.

Enamel paint on cardboard, wood, toys, furniture, clay beads. Always use unleaded paint.

Water paint on sidewalks and buildings, outside equipment, and on paper.

Paint on **clay** ready for kiln or dried clay objects.

Paint with **rollers**; use rollers with string or cord on base to create design.

Print with paints; use found objects and gadgets.

Textile paint to create wall hangings, place mats, fabric for sewing.

Blow through **straws** to create unique designs, blend colors.

Develop **new techniques**; encourage children to combine two or more ideas. Experiment with various shapes, sizes, and kinds of paper. What happens when the paper is wet or dry?

---

*See Chapter 13 on science.

Painting with Colored Ink on Cloth

White blotter
Masonite; smooth, flat board; or heavy cardboard
Cloth of thin linen, rayon, or unbleached muslin
Waterproof ink
Fine point brush or lettering pen
Pencil

Place blotter on board. Pencil design on blotter, making sure that all lines are heavy. Cut cloth large enough to cover the design and place over blotter so design shows through. Use ink sparingly—blotter will absorb surplus (large areas in the design should be covered with small strokes instead of water color wash techniques).

String Painting

Block of wood
Glue
Thick string
Cloth or paper
Tempera paint or water-soluble block-printing ink

Place several thicknesses of newspaper on table. Place glue in flat container, rub block of wood into the glue on one side. Turn block over and design the string on the glue side; leave until dry. Press design block into ink or paint and print on cloth or paper. Overprints may be made by using other blocks and designs and different color paints or inks.

Blocks can be used to make several copies, dried to use again, or string can be pulled off and another design placed on fresh glue.

Ink Painting

Paper
Water colors and brushes
Artist ink pens and ink

Children wash surface of paper with water colors or plain water, then use pen and ink to draw a design on the wet surface.

Paper

All sizes, shapes, colors, textures may be used for tearing, folding, twisting, curling, bending. Paper may be fringed, braided, scored, wrinkled, slit, bunched up, or used to weave. Crepe paper can be pulled through a hole, stretched, and used as yarn. Because paper is a natural resource, it should never be wasted.

Papier-mâché can be used for masks, jewelry, puppets, marionettes, toys, and as a base for other art media. Quick papier-mâché can be made from rolled up or folded newspapers. String is used to tie material into desired shapes that are then covered with wheat paste to which tempera coloring has been added. When almost dry, the rolls can be shaped into designs, then dried. Sometimes stapled pieces can help hold the total project together. Papier-mâché can be added around empty plastic bottles to give shape and design, then painted and shellacked.

To make papier-mâché, tear newspapers into narrow strips, about ½-inch wide, and pull them through a shallow dish containing a creamy mixture of wallpaper (wheat) paste and water. Coat the paper with the paste, and wipe off the excess with your fingers. Carefully wrap the strips around a bottle or bucket or other object. Apply approximately three layers of paper, each layer in a different direction for added strength. Be certain to smooth all cracks and loose edges on the final paper coat. Allow the paper to dry thoroughly for several days, then remove the supporting object. After the paste is dry, cover the papier-mâché with a single coat of white paint, thinned plaster, or regular white acrylic-based wall paint. Then paint designs and finish with a spray (nonaerosol) plastic, shellac, or varnish coat.

Mosaics may be made with colored pieces of paper instead of tiles.

For **strip paper sculpture**, cut paper into various widths. Bend into forms and join by staples, paste, or paper fasteners.

Newspapers can be twisted into shapes after a thin paste has been spread over them. Dry, then paint with tempera or add yarn, buttons, beads, feathers, toothpicks, etc.

Paper plates can serve as a base for masks, collages, puppets, tambourines, clocks, wall plaques, stitching designs, note holders, etc.

Sculpture

For **plaster of paris sculpture**, mix 4 cups plaster of paris with 1 quart of water. Pour into milk carton or similar container until dry and hard. Older children can remove and carve with a knife into desired design.

Soap may be used to sculpt a design and/or used as a base for sequins, beads, jewelry designs.

Sticks may be glued together to form a design. They may be constructed erect or flat on the table so pieces may be added while the project is drying.

Trips

Where can you accompany children so that they can see how art serves esthetic purposes and is used as a practical part of life? Try art galleries; art supply stores; art shows; nature walks; libraries for art and architecture books; bookstores to see prints; fabric stores to notice designs; gardens, backyards, or farmers markets to see fruits and vegetables; markets to look at designs; jewelry stores; pottery shops; puppet and marionette shows; print shops; hobby shops; and many other places where children can see art, experience it, and learn from it.

Resources

Art Guide—Let's Create a Form and *Art Guide —Let's Make a Picture*. Washington, D.C.: Association for Childhood Education International, 1969.

Barkan, M. *Through Art to Creativity*. Boston: Allyn and Bacon, 1960.

Brittain, W.L., and Lowenfeld, V. *Creative and Mental Growth*. 6th ed. New York: Macmillan, 1975.

Cardozo, P., and Menten, T. *The Whole Kids Catalog*. New York: Bantam, 1975.

Cherry, C. *Creative Art for the Developing Child*. Belmont, Calif.: Fearon, 1972.

Cobb, V. *Arts and Crafts You Can Eat*. Philadelphia: J.B. Lippincott, 1974.

Cole, N.R. *Children's Art from Deep Down Inside*. New York: John Day, 1966.

Croft, D.J., and Hess, R.D. *An Activities Handbook for Teachers of Young Children*. 2nd ed. Boston: Houghton Mifflin, 1975.

D'Amico, V.; Wilson, F.; and Maser, M. *Art for the Family*. New York: Museum of Modern Art, 1954.

Fiarotta, P. *Snips and Snails and Walnut Whales*. New York: Workman, 1975.

Fiarotta, P. *Sticks and Stones and Ice Cream Cones*. New York: Workman, 1973.

Guth, P. *Crafts for Kids*. Blue Ridge Summit, Pa.: TAB Books, 1975.

Hartley, R.E., et al. *Understanding Children's Play*. New York: Columbia University Press, 1972.

Heberholz, D., and Heberholz, B. *A Child's Pursuit of Art*. Dubuque, Iowa: William C. Brown, 1967.

Krevitsky, N. *Batik Art and Craft*. rev. ed. Cincinnati, Ohio: Van Nostrand Reinhold, 1973.

Linderman, E.W., and Linderman, M.M. *Crafts for the Classroom*. New York: Macmillan, 1977.

Linse, B.B. *Arts and Crafts for All Seasons*. Belmont, Calif.: Fearon, 1969.

Maile, A. *Tie and Dye as a Present Day Craft*. New York: Taplinger, 1971.

Meilach, D.Z. *Contemporary Batik and Tie-Dye Methods*. New York: Crown, 1973.

Pattemore, A.W. *Art and Environment: An Art Resource for Teachers*. Cincinnati, Ohio: Van Nostrand Reinhold, 1974.

Sattler, H.R. *Recipes for Art and Craft Materials*. New York: Lothrop, Lee & Shepard, 1973.

Wankelman, W., et al. *A Handbook of Arts and Crafts for Elementary and Junior High School Teachers*. 3rd ed. Dubuque, Iowa: William C. Brown, 1974.

Weiss, H. *Collage and Construction*. Reading, Mass.: Addison-Wesley, 1970.

Weiss, H. *Paper, Ink and Roller*. Reading, Mass.: Addison-Wesley, 1958.

Wendorff, R. *How to Make Cornhusk Dolls*. New York: Arco, 1973.

Whitman Creative Art Books. Racine, Wisc.: Whitman, 1967.

Wiseman, A. *Making Things: The Hand Book of Creative Discovery*. Boston: Little, Brown, 1973.

Construction helps children learn how to size up problems and to figure out ways of dealing with the problem.

28

Blocks 5

Blocks and children go together as naturally as sleighs and winter or apples and pie. The earnest concentration and the lively conversations of children playing with blocks make this very clear, as do the frequent shouts of "See what I made" and "Look what we built." Why are blocks fun for children, and why are they an important part of an educational program?

Blocks give children opportunities to become masters of space and materials as they build towers of hollow blocks, bridges with arches and columns that span the room, or tiny structures with small table blocks, big enough for only one doll or matchbox car. There are opportunities to create: roads for cars to travel on, hideouts or clubhouses to escape to, buildings to play house in, cages to contain scary monsters, rockets and spaceships for trips to outer space, and castles to live in. Children can be caught up in the beauty of shape, balance, and color as they constantly change what they are building and add decorations. There are times when everybody wants to help with the project; this creates opportunities for the children to share feelings of satisfaction, achievement, and cooperation.

While it is fun to see the finished product, there is just as much pleasure in the process of creating it. Tearing it down and starting over again is very much a part of this, for although blocks themselves are solid, they are as flexible in use as the child's imagination. There is no one way to use blocks; children of all ages may work near each other, a mighty fortress may rise right beside a flat, row-of-blocks road.

By lifting, carrying, bending, reaching, grasping, holding, and pushing blocks of all kinds, children have opportunities to develop large and small muscles, and muscular coordination. At the same time, delicately adding one more block to a tower, sliding a car in and out of an archway, or getting more blocks without bumping everything down, helps children sharpen hand-eye coordination.

Children can learn new words by using and naming ramps, pillars, arches, cylinders, and cubes. They can also learn to tell other children their ideas, needs, and wishes—"That's mine," "I'll trade you things," "If you put that there, it will fall down." As they play with blocks, children can learn a great deal about getting along with others of all ages—such as respecting the ideas and property of others, waiting for and taking turns, sharing, and compromising. Construction helps children learn how to size up problems—for example, that the roof planks are too short for the building—and to figure out ways of dealing with the problem—using different roofing materials, moving the walls closer together, eliminating the roof. With blocks, children have wonderful opportunities for make-believe as they change and extend their dramatic play and for converting the vast world around them into a smaller, more manageable one by building and using approximations of the objects in that world: roads, stores, train stations, bridges, walls, space modules. Using the many different kinds of blocks, accessories, and surroundings that are part of this kind of play, children can begin to understand such abstractions as:

Shape—by using rectangular, triangular, cylindrical, and cone-shaped blocks and large and small cubes.

Space—by making buildings big enough to get into, or perhaps only big enough for the pet mouse, or by building in large yards or in smaller rooms among other children.

Height—by building flat roads, ranch houses, or skyscrapers.

Similarities and differences—by looking for a certain kind of block to plug a hole in an almost-finished wall, or by sorting blocks into groups and putting them back where they belong.

Numbers and mathematical relationships—by counting blocks, placing two half-size blocks together to make a whole block, placing two blocks

29

together to make a double block, or even by feeling that there are "too many" to pick up alone at cleanup time.

Safety—by building out of the way of doors and places where people walk, lining up corners for sturdiness, and staying within certain limits. But the limits should be based on the kind of space, number and ages of the children, and what they have already demonstrated they can handle. Limits should not be arbitrary.

Children have opportunities to wonder, experiment, discover, master materials, and assume responsibilities when they build with blocks.

Permanent Equipment

We recommend the following as a minimum for groups of 15 children.

Floor blocks—approximately 480 pieces
28 pillars
28 half-units
192 units
100 double units
48 quadruple units
20 roofing boards
20 ramps
12 triangles
8 arches
8 quarter-circle arches
2 half-circle arches
1 Y switch
1 X switch
12 large cylinders

Hollow blocks
12 units
18 double units
6 quadruple units
6 cleated boards
12 plain boards

Parquetry blocks

Wood-snap blocks

Table blocks—design blocks, plastic blocks, opensided blocks

Addition cubes, dominoes

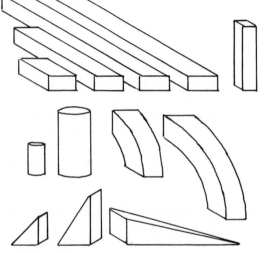
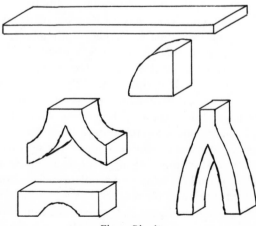

Floor Blocks

Learning Materials

Transportation and dramatic play—sturdy plastic and wooden cars, carts, steering wheels, delivery trucks, school buses, firetrucks, boats, jeeps, planes, helicopters, trains, freight, passengers, wheelbarrows, tricycles, wagons, derricks, roadmaking equipment, bell for train, megaphone, play money, engineer's hats, paper for tickets, discarded license plates, cash register boxes, ladders, heavy cardboard for roofs, telephones, dashboard, boards for counters in train stations, traffic signs.

People and animals—plastic or rubber community people of various ages, ethnic groups, and occupations; domestic animals.

Miscellaneous—rugs, blankets, tarpaulin, clothespins, telephone wire, string, pieces of rubber tubes, spools, cans, cones, wheels, old radios, empty food cartons, paper boxes, hats and clothing, gas and air pumps, fences, freeway maps, architecture books, storybooks.

Storage

Items should be adjacent to area for block play or carrying carts should be available.

Shelves, baskets, boxes, cabinets, wood box on casters, labeled for organized storage.

Shelves should be open face for easy accessibility—division of shelves with boards helps keep like blocks together.

If material is stored outdoors, make sure it is protected from wet ground surfaces and damage from water play or rain.

TOPICS TO TALK ABOUT WITH CHILDREN

Size, shape, and function—rectangular, triangular, cubical, spherical, cylindrical, circular, curve, elliptical curve, circular arch, small circle, ramps, buttress, floor board, pillar, Y switch, X switch, roofing boards, units, double units, quadruple units, Gothic arch, Gothic door.

Determining best organization of blocks on shelves, in boxes, cabinets, baskets.

Various ways of transporting blocks from one area to another.

Children can plan for what is to be built: What blocks will be needed, what space is available, who will work with the blocks, how much time is there, what accessory materials are available?

Safety—can large blocks be perched on a small base? Is the available space adequate for the structure? Is it out of traffic lanes?

Children can take photographs of their structures. What was built? What else might be added? What other blocks or accessories might be used?

Children can develop new ideas on trips taken to see interesting buildings, freeways, lumberyards, construction equipment.

What are the economics and politics involved in construction? Discuss local problems and progress.

Explore the variety of occupations available in the construction industry. Talk with workers to learn more about how they fit into the total process.

IDEAS TO TRY

Encourage children to label buildings, numbers, street name, building name, etc.

Tape trips to the lumberyard, brickyard, city hall, banks, markets, airport, department stores.

Children can sand blocks as needed to keep them free of splinters.

Initiate a discussion about new construction activity, and go for a walking trip. Take along a camera, steel tape measure, paper, pencils, and small rulers, tape recorder (some of the workers may agree to an interview). Upon returning, older children can make scale blueprints on graph paper, using their measurements of the construction site. Architects' blueprints, children's sketches and photographs, can be displayed in the center. Encourage construction, story writing, and discussion about the project.

Revisit the site to observe progress. In this activity, children are:

- exploring concepts of size, shape, balance, length, width, volume, measurement, charting, and mapping.

- expanding language experience through story writing, problem solving, interviewing, and discussion.

- creating a personalized view of reality through construction and reproduction.

- mastering a task by undertaking a worthwhile project and seeing it through to completion.

Children may discover that the blocks on hand are not adequate for reproducing the desired construction. Extend the activity into the woodworking area, where the children can measure, saw, and sand their own blocks for completion of the project.

There are times when everybody wants to help with the project; this creates opportunities for the children to share feelings of achievement, satisfaction, and cooperation.

Resources

Antin, C. "Blocks in the Curriculum." New York: Early Childhood Education Council of New York, 1952.

Franklin, A. "Blocks, A Tool of Learning." New York: Bank Street College of Education, 1960.

Hartley, R.E., et al. *Understanding Children's Play*. New York: Columbia University Press, 1952.

Hirsch, E.S., ed. *The Block Book*. Washington, D.C.: National Association for the Education of Young Children, 1974.

Johnson, H.M. "The Art of Block Building." New York: Bank Street College of Education, 1933.

Lambert, H.M. *Teaching the Kindergarten Child.* New York: Harcourt, Brace, 1958.

Leonard, E., et al. *Foundations of Learning in Child Education*. Columbus, Ohio: Charles E. Merrill, 1963.

Rudolph, M., and Cohen, D.H. *Kindergarten: A Year of Learning*. New York: Appleton-Century-Crofts, 1964.

Rudolph, M., and Cohen, D.H. "The Many Purposes of Blockbuilding and Woodwork." *Young Children* 20, no. 1 (October 1964): 40-46.

Shoemaker, R.M. "All in Play." New York: Play School Association, 1958.

Dramatic Play and Creative Dramatics

6

A child climbing over boxes and putting out a make-believe fire; a make-believe cowboy riding a barrel as if it were a bucking bronco; a child setting a make-believe dinner table or cuddling a baby doll; these are examples of dramatic play, an important part of children's programs.

Dramatic play is a ticket to anywhere—the moon, a castle—it gives children a chance to step out of their own lives and become other people for a while. The shy, quiet child can become a snarling lion in the wild animal show. The child who usually follows directions can become a construction supervisor, directing a large project. Dramatic play is fast-moving and original, managed by the children themselves. It stands magically apart from grownups' rules and schedules, yet gives children power to do all the things they see adults do: buying, selling, directing, traveling, rewarding, and punishing.

Dressing up in fancy clothes, such as ballet costumes, space helmets and goggles, floppy hats, and capes, is fun and lets children try things that might be scary in real life. Destroying snakes and monsters, whining and crying like a baby, or being mean mothers, fathers, or teachers, allows children to release strong feelings and express pressing needs to be powerful, aggressive, brave, strong, or helpless. Sometimes dramatic play is a good way to relive happy experiences, and sometimes it is a comforting way to make up for parts of a day that have not been so good.

Playing the youngest child in the family, the busy mother, or the tough police officer may help children see things from someone else's point of view and help them understand why people act the way they do. Playing newspaper reporters, gas station attendants, secretaries, or letter carriers helps children increase their understanding of what really happens in the grownup world. For example, they learn that reporters interview people and write stories. Coworkers take photographs, design layouts, print copy, and sell a finished product. Some kinds of dramatic play help children work through frightening, embarrassing, or unhappy experiences they have had and come to solutions that are helpful to them in facing similar situations.

Dramatic play sometimes requires groups of children to push heavy boxes or build up the fort or round up enough friends to make a patrol. This helps children learn that sometimes people need and depend on one another. It also helps children learn to work together: sharing, taking turns, waiting, dividing responsibilities, and accepting rules such as using words to express ideas, wants, plans, and feelings. It encourages children to learn more descriptive words and shows them that language is important if they want to be heard and understood.

More mature children will engage in dramatic play such as pretending to live like people from other countries, which requires planning ahead and making special props like clothes or food. Other play, such as rescuing wildlife from an oil slick or a polluted river, may be less complicated, but all of these things encourage children to take an interest in the wider world. They also create wonderful opportunities for children to read or write stories, poems, or books about what they are doing. Dramatic play gives children wonderful incentives to find out more about the things they are interested in.

Dramatic play not only provides opportunities for learning about unfamiliar situations, it also provides a unique opportunity for children to begin to become aware of themselves—their bodies, their thoughts, and their feelings. One way to open these avenues to children is through the use of creative dramatics.

Creative dramatics is a more mature form of the spontaneous dramatic play of young children. Group activities such as story improvisations, body movement, and pantomime give older children a chance to articulate their thoughts and feelings and to socialize and work together toward a common goal. These activities also stimulate ideas and creativity and give children experience in problem solving.

Children enjoy improvising and may be motivated to do so through their own experiences, music, art, or a story which captures their attention. The following suggestions may help you as you assist children in developing their improvisations.

You or one of the children may wish to select a story, either to be told or read by an adult or an older child. Care should be taken to select a clear and meaningful plot in which the characters are consistent and human. A limited number of incidents leading to a quick and satisfying ending would be best, especially for beginners.

In telling the story, you should be familiar with the material, retaining picturesque or humorous words or phrases. Telling the story clearly and in a natural way by making eye contact with the children will create more interest. Narration can be converted to dialogue, and characters should be suggested but not played. Pauses and changes in volume and rhythm can build toward the climax.

Children can do much of the planning, character selection, and scene re-creation. Adults can be available to assist by asking questions to encourage children to expand their play. Individual characters can be stimulated to think about their roles: Where have you seen an eagle? What did its face look like? How did its head move? How can you show feathers? How do eagles carry themselves? What color are they?

Guidance may be necessary as each scene is developed. How does the scene start? What is the main conflict? What is each of the characters doing? What happened right before the scene?

After the children have completed the improvisation, they may wish to discuss and evaluate it, possibly reading the story upon which it was based or writing to record dialogue and costumes used. Children can discuss their favorite parts, and may wish to relate the improvisation to situations they have encountered. Suggestions for improvements might be implemented.

Learning Equipment and Materials

Children enjoy improvising and creativity can be stimulated by making a few materials available. You may wish to select a few items from these lists to encourage dramatic play.

Basic Play

Boxes	Spools
Boards	Pipe cleaners
Barrels	Wallets
Planks (short and long)	Purses
Ladders	Shoes
Packing crates	Hats
Cargo nets	Coats
Blocks	Scarves
Sawhorses	Long skirts
Horizontal ladders	Gloves
Tires	Old lace curtains
Tubes	Sheets
Yarn	Belts
Scissors	Shirts
Cloth	Suspenders
Needles	Neckties
Thread	Bits of bright fabrics
Buttons	Ribbons
Beads	Laces
Bits of leather	Small mirrors
Plastic cloth	Jewelry
Oilcloth	Artificial flowers
	Cheesecloth

Family

Plastic pans for washing babies or dishes	Suitcases
Towels and washcloths	Tablecloths
Dish towels	Napkins
Dishes	Clothesline
Eating utensils	Clothespins
Cans of food	Dust pan
Pots and pans	Mixing spoons
Telephones	Clock
Floor mops	Lunch kits
Brooms	Dolls
	Furniture

Medical

Stethoscopes	Doctor bag
Plastic hypos	Flashlight
Nurses' caps	Magazines
Aprons	Wagons
Lab coats	Admittance forms
Band-Aids	Watch
Gauze	Bottles
Adhesive tape	

Office

Telephones	Calendars
Telephone book	Pens
File	Cash register
Material to file	Drafting board
Manila folders	Adding machine
Envelopes	Briefcase
Notepads	Stapler
Pencils	Stamps
Wastebasket	Hole puncher
Typewriter	Printing set
Order books	

34

Children enjoy improvising and may be motivated to do so through their own experiences, music, art, or a story which captures their attention.

Beautician

Hair clips	Orange sticks
Rollers	Oil for cuticles
Bobby pins	Hand lotion
Combs	Soap
Cotton puffs	Hand mirror
Powder boxes	Towels
Plastic caps	Nail polish
Emery boards	Bottles

Store

Cash register	Items for sale
Scale	Baskets
Play money	Shopping bags

Firefighter

Hats	Wheel
Ladders	Wagons
Bell	Hose

Gas Station

Gas cans	Tire pump
Oil cans	Gas pump
Tools	Cash register
Tool box	Road maps
Rags	Steering wheel
Hose	Play money

Bus or Train

Money changer	Lunch box
Tickets	Newspaper
Ticket punch	

Construction

Rope and pulley	Shovels
Plastic buckets	Steamroller
Pipes for water	Trucks
Hose	Wheelbarrow

Storage

Boxes, shelves, drawers, cabinets, baskets, hooks, all labeled to facilitate return and retrieval.

Items should be stored near the area in which they are most likely to be used; portable units may be necessary for some items.

Personal property in temporary use should be marked.

TOPICS TO TALK ABOUT WITH CHILDREN

Skills used in various dramatic play situations.

Originality, imagination, inventiveness—new ways of doing things, how people do things in different ways.

Props children can make themselves—puppet theater, puppets, dressup clothes.

Items children can bring from home to supplement props for dramatic play.

Stories, poems, books, pictures, films, filmstrips, television, and radio—what children watch and listen to at home.

School trips they have taken or plan to take.

Freedoms and limitations—children's responsibilities to follow through on safety, care, and replacement of materials.

The children themselves—what they would enjoy doing, how they feel, places they have visited with their families, places they have lived, what they do on weekends.

Portable Storage Unit

People—where they work, what they do, how they dress, what they eat, how they play, where they live, how they are similar and different, how they are dependent on one another.

Current events—in the center, neighborhood, city, state, country, world—as they relate to children's play, interest, and understanding.

IDEAS TO TRY

Children can make hideouts, houses, tents, caves, forts, or stores from sheets, blankets, rugs, painter's drop cloths, tarpaulins.

Help children cut holes in cardboard boxes for crawl-through equipment. Cut top and bottom out of a large cardboard box and cut down on one side to make a four-panel screen; use as house, store, post office.

Old appliances and mechanical parts can be mounted on boards for use as control units, dashboards.

Spaceships can be made by children from tall fiberboard tubes with the nose cone from a sheet of lightweight cardboard. Cover windows with cellophane, transparent plastic wrap, tissue paper, waxed paper. Five-gallon ice cream containers are perfect for space hats.

Stack tires for a hiding place or a house; make climbing equipment by tying three or four tires together side by side and then tying each end to a tree or post.

A trampoline can be constructed from a tire and canvas; stretch canvas taut and carefully bolt to the tire.

Tree houses can be built by the children with different ways to get up and down: rope ladders, logs, boxes, planks, steps, rocks.

Wigs can be made from wool, raffia, and pulled crepe paper.

For original costumes, children can crayon designs on fabric and iron between sheets of absorbent paper.

Coins and money can be made from paper, cardboard, aluminum foil, papier-mâché, clay.

Paper flowers and papier-mâché jewelry can be made to sell in play stores; display in boxes, on shelves, on tables.

Have children plan a circus. Make pompoms, hats, costumes for a parade, masks, animal cages, banners. Sell popcorn, tickets.

Children can make musical instruments, march as a band, use a variety of instruments for an orchestra.

Make totem poles from cardboard boxes for an Indian village; make clothing from unbleached muslin, headbands from leather, moccasins from leather, jewelry from clay. Join three poles together at top and cover with burlap bags to make a home.

Help children make street signs, signals, prices for merchandise, address signs.

Talk with parents about discarded items children can bring from home.

Visit gas stations for old tires and tubes; telephone company for telephones and large wire wheels from cables; television stores for large cardboard boxes and old television cabinets; aircraft salvage departments for a variety of mechanical devices, boxes, crates, cabinets, and parts; markets for crates, boxes, and posters.

Visit airline offices for maps, time schedules, hats, wings, and carry bags; furniture stores for rug samples, fabric samples, and packing crates; junkyards for years, steering wheels, keys, and dashboards.

Children can construct a large animal from a sawhorse or by putting a log across two sawhorses. Add head, tail, and mane for a horse; carpet and upholstery samples to make a woolly sheep; horns or antlers to make a mythical beast.

Accompany a group of children to the library for selection of a play or a story they wish to enact.

Encourage older children to read to younger children and to help facilitate creative play.

Ask a local performer to demonstrate skills and assist children in their development.

Resources

Chambers, D.W. *Storytelling and Creative Drama.* Dubuque, Iowa: William C. Brown, 1970.

"Creating with Materials for Work and Play." Washington, D.C.: Association for Childhood Education International, 1969.

Ehrlich, H., ed. *Creative Dramatics Handbook.* Urbana, Ill.: National Council of Teachers of English, 1974.

Gardner, R. *Costumes for All Ages, All Occasions.* New York: David McKay, 1970.

Gillies, E. *Creative Dramatics for Children.* Washington, D.C.: Association for Childhood Education International, 1973.

Hartley, R. E., et al. *Understanding Children's Play.* New York: Columbia University Press, 1952.

Housing for Early Childhood Education—Centers for Growing and Learning. Washington, D.C.: Association for Childhood Education International, 1968.

Law, N.R., and Wu, H.C. "Equipment: Challenge or Stereotype?" *Young Children* 20, no. 1 (October 1964): 18-24.

Leonard, E., et al. *Foundations of Learning in Child Education.* Columbus, Ohio: Charles E. Merrill, 1963.

McCaslin, N. *Creative Dramatics in the Classroom.* 2nd ed. New York: David McKay, 1974.

Moncure, J.B. "Something Out of Nothing." *Young Children* 20, no. 1 (October 1964): 38-39.

Perryman, L.C. "Dramatic Play and Cognitive Development." New York: Bank Street College of Education, Publication #22, 1962.

Pile, N.F. *Art Experiences for Young Children.* Vol. 5. Threshold Early Learning Library. New York: Macmillan, 1973.

Rudolph, M., and Cohen, D.H. *Kindergarten: A Year of Learning.* New York: Appleton-Century-Crofts, 1964.

Scarfe, N. N. "Play Is Education." *Childhood Education* 39, no. 3 (November 1962): 117-121.

Shaftel, F.R., and Shaftel, G. *Role-Playing for Social Values.* Englewood Cliffs, N.J.: Prentice-Hall, 1967.

Silks, G.B. *Drama with Children.* New York: Harper & Row, 1977.

Siks, G.B., and Dunnington, H.B., eds. *Children's Theater and Creative Dramatics.* Seattle: University of Washington Press, 1961.

Snook, B. *Costumes for Children.* Newton Centre, Mass.: Charles T. Branford, 1970.

Spolin, V. *Improvisation for the Theatre.* Evanston, Ill.: Northwestern University Press, 1963.

Taylor, K.W. *Parents and Children Learn Together.* 2nd ed. New York: Columbia University Press, 1968.

Todd, V.E., and Heffernan, H. *The Years Before School: Guiding Preschool Children.* 2nd ed. New York: Macmillan, 1970.

Ward, W. *Playmaking with Children from Kindergarten Through Junior High School.* 2nd ed. New York: Appleton-Century-Crofts, 1957.

Puppets and Marionettes

7

A group of children whisper excitedly as they wait for their friends to begin a puppet show. A couple of children giggle as they make their puppets yawn or fall down. A child with a puppet on each hand smiles as he makes the puppets talk to each other. Why are puppets an important part of programs for children?

Dressed in brightly colored costumes, falling down and popping up again, making jokes —puppets are beautiful and fun to watch. Children putting on puppet shows hear their friends laughing and clapping, and they have a chance to feel successful, powerful, funny, and entertaining. Hidden by the curtain during a puppet show or just sitting on a rug playing with puppets, children create their own world of make-believe—"You be the frog and I'll be the princess." "I'm going to be silly." With puppets, children can do things that might be embarrassing or frightening in real life. For the children using the puppets as well as for the children watching, puppets are a ticket to a different world.

As they make puppets kick their legs, nod their heads, wave their arms, open their mouths, and whisk back and forth, children develop hand-eye coordination and learn to use their small muscles skillfully. Making puppets speak so the audience can hear and understand them helps children learn to speak clearly.

Carefully following the story and the action of the puppets requires children to learn to listen carefully. Acting the part of the shy, angry, silly, mean, kind, stuck-up, scared, or brave puppet gives children a chance to find out about their own and other people's feelings. It gives them a chance to test feelings and responses in different situations—"I'm scared so I'll hide." "I like you, so I'll hug you."

Playing with puppets and putting on shows gives children opportunities to work together and to solve problems—"You can come in after my puppet falls down." "How can we make a big enough stage for all of us to fit behind?" With puppets, children can make up stories from their own experiences. They also can be encouraged to read books, poems, and songs to get ideas to use with their puppets. Puppet shows to be presented before an audience give children the opportunity to learn how to plan for the time length of the show and for the beginning, the exciting part, and the end of the story. Children can write what everyone is going to say, and can make signs announcing the show. Some shows are made up as they go along instead of being carefully planned; in both kinds there are wonderful opportunities for children to imagine, to dream, to think about possibilities and realities, and then to put these ideas into words and actions that can be shared with others.

Learning Materials

Bags—all sizes
Balloons
Balls
Beads
Boxes—all shapes and sizes
Broom straws
Brushes—assorted sizes and shapes
Buttons, button molds
Cans—all sizes and shapes
Cardboard
Clay
Cloth—all colors, sizes, textures
Cork
Cotton batting
Crayons
Curtains and curtain rods
Doweling
Embroidery and sewing thread
Feathers
Felt
Felt pens

Foil
Gloves
Glue
Gourds
Hammer, nails, and screws
Handkerchiefs
Hooks and eyes, snaps
Jewelry
Kapok
Lace
Lace doilies
Leather
Magazines
Masonite
Needles
Nylon hose
Paints—tempera and enamel
Paper—wrapping, cleansing tissue, construction, cardboard tubing and cones, contact, corrugated, gift wrap, graph, napkins, newspaper, telephone books, towel
Paper fasteners
Papier-mâché
Paste
Pencils
Pins
Pipe cleaners
Plastic wood
Plywood
Raffia
Ribbons
Rope
Rubber bands
Sawdust
Scissors
Screens
Shellac or lacquer
Shoelaces
Socks
Sponges
Spools
Stapler

Sticks
String—all colors and weights
Styrofoam
Tape
Thumbtacks
Tongue depressors
Trimmings—all kinds
Tulle
Turpentine
Window shades
Wire—thin
Wire coathangers
Yardstick
Zippers

Acting the part of a puppet gives children a chance to find out about their own and other people's feelings.

Cardboard or cloth hanging shoe organizers.

Cardboard or plastic shoe boxes.

TOPICS TO TALK ABOUT WITH CHILDREN

Which kind of puppet or marionette would best fit the character?

How to care for puppets and marionettes.

Color, size, shape, texture, and other variations of materials which can be used for making puppets, marionettes, and stages.

Books, stories, poetry, and songs that can be reenacted with puppets and marionettes.

How to manipulate puppets and marionettes to create the story and express feeling.

Integration of the many media needed for puppetry.

Children can develop plans for coordination of characters, language, setting, scenery.

Storage

Boxes, shelves, baskets, cabinets, cupboards, drawers, labeled. Shelves of different heights and widths to accommodate puppets, marionettes, and accessory materials.

Plastic bags, closed containers for puppets and marionettes, labeled.

Trips to puppet shows at public libraries or amusement parks.

IDEAS TO TRY

Design and make many different kinds of puppets—paper bag, stick, rod, shadow, cardboard, sock, glove, finger, folded paper, handkerchief or other cloth over fist, twig, box, felt.

Design and make marionettes using a variety of materials for head and bodies—papier-mâché, crushed paper, styrofoam, wood, boxes of all sizes and shapes, clay, stocking over kapok, hinged or strung.

Make and design costumes utilizing art and sewing skills.

Observe and design puppets and costumes that represent community workers, fantasy people and animals, storybook figures, circus clowns and animals, ethnic groups.

Develop original dialogue or use a favorite story or poem as a base.

Plan and make props, stage scenery for puppet theater.

Design and make a puppet theatre. It can be impromptu or more permanent, simple or complex. Use carpentry tools.

Sew curtains and develop ways to open and close curtains.

Make storage boxes for puppets, marionettes, costumes, props, etc.

Plan and make posters for publicity for puppet presentation, using creative art experiences.

Take trips to commercial puppet theaters; see amateur performances at schools, community playgrounds, and libraries.

Resources

Adair, M.W. *Do-It-In-A-Day Puppets: For Beginners*. New York: John Day, 1964.

Alkema, C.J. *Puppet-Making*. New York: Sterling, 1971.

Andersen, B.E. *Let's Start a Puppet Theatre*. Cincinnati, Ohio: Van Nostrand Reinhold, 1973.

Baird, B. *The Art of the Puppet*. Boston: Plays, 1966.

Batchelder, M.H. *The Puppet Theatre Handbook*. New York: Harper & Row, 1974.

Batchelder, M.H., and Comer, V.L. *Puppets and Plays: A Creative Approach*. New York: Harper & Row, 1956.

Bates, E. *Potpourri of Puppetry*. Canyon, Texas: West Texas State University, 1974.

Currell, D. *Puppetry for School Children*. Newton Centre, Mass.: Charles T. Branford, 1970.

Hanford, R.T. *The Complete Book of Puppets and Puppeteering*. New York: Drake, 1976.

Howard, V. *Puppet and Pantomime Plays*. New York: Sterling, 1971.

Kampmann, R. *Creating with Puppets*. Cincinnati, Ohio: Van Nostrand Reinhold, 1972.

Lee, M. *Puppet Theatre*. Fair Lawn, N.J.: Essential Books, 1958.

Lewis, S., and Oppenheimer, L. *Folding Paper Puppets*. New York: Stein and Day, 1962.

Linderman, E.W., and Linderman, M.M. *Crafts for the Classroom*. New York: Macmillan, 1977.

Mahlmann, L., and Jones, D.C. *Puppet Plays for Young Players*. Boston: Plays, 1974.

Niculescu, M. *The Puppet Theatre of the Modern World*. Boston: Plays, 1967.

Pels, G. *Easy Puppets*. New York: Thomas Y. Crowell, 1951.

Peyton, J. *Puppetry—A Tool for Teaching: A Guide for Teachers on the Use of Puppetry in Education*. New Haven, Conn.: Bojabi Tree and the Theater of Education and Puppetry Arts, 1975.

Philpott, A.R. *Let's Look at Puppets*. Racine, Wisc.: Whitman, 1966.

Richter, D. *Fell's Guide to Hand Puppets*. New York: Frederick Fell, 1970.

Ross, L. *Finger Puppets: Easy to Make and Fun to Use*. New York: Lothrop, Lee & Shepard, 1971.

Ross, L. *Puppet Shows Using Poems and Stories*. New York: Lothrop, Lee & Shepard, 1970.

Ward, W. *Playmaking with Children from Kindergarten Through Junior High School*. 2nd ed. New York: Appleton-Century-Crofts, 1957.

42   *The center day can begin and end with music. Small groups of children and staff may gather informally for a round of favorite songs.*

Music and Dance 8

The special joys of music and dance should be a part of each day for children. Music offers so many things—the pleasure of singing favorite songs with friends or of musing and dreaming while listening to a record, the exhilaration of folk dances, the excitement of creating one's own dance. Music is a wonderful outlet for feelings of joy, sorrow, or anger. It encourages children to express their feelings creatively and gives them a sense of belonging.

The center day can begin and end with music. Small groups of children and staff may gather informally for a round of favorite songs. Accompaniment is not essential; if a staff member or older child can play the piano, guitar, or other instrument, this adds to the enjoyment. Children and adults can quickly learn to accompany themselves on an autoharp.

Every child has favorite songs and keeps adding to the collection: songs that tickle the funny bone—"I Know an Old Lady Who Swallowed a Fly"; songs that quicken a sense of beauty—"Oh, How Lovely Is the Evening"; or songs that start the child off on a lively march—"Stars and Stripes Forever."

Music of different cultures and countries should be part of each child's experience. Folk songs and dances from around the world provide a natural outlet for children's expanding interest in other people and countries; melodies and rhythms have universal appeal.

Children's ears are tuned to the beat of rock and soul music, and to exclude this form of contemporary musical expression from the center would be a denial of an important part of their environment. It is good for children to have a chance to compare many kinds of musical expression. The acid rock singing groups of the sixties have given way to a whole new generation of music, which is more directly influenced by jazz, calypso, and folk music. Ask children to share their favorites with you; meanwhile, start listening to the radio yourself. You'll be surprised. The new rock sounds a lot like the old jazz. Capitalize on children's fervent interest in contemporary rock music and use it in many ways.

Language learnings in music are evident in expanded vocabularies. The more children sing, the better they may read, speak, and listen. Older children can read directions for making instruments and can be helpful to younger children.

Hand in hand with singing goes dance. There should be opportunities for many kinds of body movement experiences in the all-day program. The familiar pleasures of folk dancing should be balanced with chances to explore other ways of moving arms and legs and bodies. Encourage children to use the tom-tom to create rhythmic patterns which will lead them to create their own dances. Dance with them and encourage them to respond to rhythm and music in their own unique manner. You will not need many props—plenty of space, indoors and out, and a tom-tom will suffice to begin with. Later on, you can add some of the accessories suggested; hoops to roll and scarves or crepe paper streamers to twirl are especially versatile for children.

The more children move, the better they move; the better they know what they can do with their bodies, the better they use their bodies to communicate feelings and ideas. And they love doing it.

When children get excited about music, it spills over into the whole program. Soon they will be creating their own rhythm instruments and their own songs. Parents will catch this excitement, too. Late afternoon sings can be family affairs, with parents joining in as they arrive to pick up their children. Many parents have musical talents; a visit from a parent to share and play an instrument or to sing is a never-to-be-forgotten treat and a wonderful way of learning about music.

It is important to have good commercial musical instruments and equipment so that children can learn to recognize fine tone quality. Whether children use commercial instruments or create their own, the following criteria apply:

- Instruments should have good tone quality so that they make a real musical contribution, not just noise.
- Instruments should be attractive and durable.
- Instruments from various cultural groups should be as authentic as possible.

Permanent Equipment

Autoharp
Bells—sleigh bells, temple bells, jingle bells, wrist bells, resonator bells
Books—poetry, song, and story
Castanets
Chinese temple blocks
Clogs
Cymbals—hand and finger
Drums—American Indian, bongo, floor, hand rhythm, tom-tom
Films and filmstrips
Guitar
Maracas and maraca sticks
Piano
Pictures
Record player
Records—classical, ethnic, holiday, marches, movement, singing, rhythm instruments, rock
Recorders
Rhythm sticks—wooden, bamboo, some fringed at ends
Tambourines
Tape recorder and tapes
Triangle and striker

The familiar pleasures of folk dancing should be balanced with chances to explore other ways of moving arms and legs and bodies.

Learning Materials

Balloons
Balls—light and heavy
Beanbags
Cloth—various sizes, shapes, and textures
Dressup clothes
Hoops
Jouncing boards

Pompoms
Ribbons
Rolled-up newspapers—fringed on one end, secured with elastic band
Ropes—clothesline, jump rope
Scarves
Streamers

Storage

Labeled boxes, bags, and baskets which can be used indoors or outdoors.

Pegboard and hooks for rhythm instruments, dressup clothing, hoops.

Portable labeled shelving units that can be moved about the room or pushed out of the way.

Clothesline and clothespins for hanging up costumes.

Record cabinet in which records are organized for quick selection.

Music books on specially marked bookshelves.

Picture file organized for easy access.

TOPICS TO TALK ABOUT WITH CHILDREN

Observations made on a trip. What was most interesting? What did they see, hear, touch?

Different ways to move from one place to another —"Can you slide over to the other side of the room with long and short slides?"

Body balance—what happens when the child stands or hops on one foot or leans forward or backward or far to the side.

Space, self in space, direction—right and left, up and down, in front of and behind, over and under, far and near, high and low.

Sizes, shapes, colors, textures—relate the discussion to visible things in the environment.

Differentiating sounds—the sound of a slight pounding of a drum and a large bang.

Feelings children experience when they hear soft, loud, fast, or slow music; lullabies; marches. How people feel and express their feelings through different media and in different ways.

Listening—following directions in making instruments, identifying types of sounds or instruments, learning words and melodies of new songs.

Choosing which songs to sing, records to play, materials to use.

Names, uses, categories, sounds, and parts of instruments; functions of parts of a record player; looking at the vibrating strings of a piano.

Care of instruments. Which ones require special efforts?

New sounds heard on the way to school or on the way home or on a visit. What do these sounds tell you?

Folk dances children enjoy doing. What do they mean to the cultures from which they come?

IDEAS TO TRY

Listen to birds singing, dogs barking, rain falling, rhythm of feet when walking, clock ticking, bells ringing, people talking, ocean waves falling, hands clapping, instruments being played, car horns tooting, children playing, mothers calling, water running, doorbells ringing, ice cream vendors calling, airplanes zooming, babies crying, skirts swishing, bees humming, etc.

Listen for loud and soft sounds, quick and slow sounds, differences and similarities in sounds.

Listen to lullabies and marches, ethnic folk music, restful music, music for movement and rhythm instruments.

Move to sounds of drums and rattles, combining movement with playing instruments and singing.

Use good rhythm instruments to develop musical appreciation. Have fun making music and doing body movements with childmade instruments—shakers, drums, tambourines, rhythm sticks, fringed bamboo sticks—and with simple instruments like castanets.

Use props for enhancing movement. Find different ways to use materials and equipment such as balls, balloons, streamers, and scarves.

Tap drum to sound like thunder and then tap to sound like falling rain.

Tape rhythm sticks together, tap sticks on floor, rug, wood, metal, cloth, tambourine.

Try moving body to poetry—running, leaping, skipping, walking slowly or rapidly, sliding, twisting, twirling.

Create tunes, songs, movement actions in many different ways.

Try sounds out on the piano; watch the hammers move as keys are struck.

Make up new sounds, new ways to move. Combine sounds and movement in ways you think will be fun.

When children get excited about music, it spills over into the whole program. Soon they will be creating their own rhythm instruments and their own songs.

Try to recognize instruments being used in records you are playing.

Take turns playing instruments, clapping while others play or dance.

Make a scrapbook of pictures—instruments, dancing, musical centers visited, concert halls, open air dances.

Accompany children to various performances—concerts, recitals, musicals. Discuss different types of music and dance and what moods are created by them.

45

Encourage children to take dancing or instrumental lessons at their schools and to share their talents with the other children.

Assist children if necessary in writing their own music or creating their own interpretive dance.

Explore communication through pantomime.

How is music used to create a mood? Listen to commercials, television shows.

Ask people in various music careers to visit the center, or visit them while they are at work—concert musicians, record store clerks, dancers at rehearsals, disc jockeys, composers.

Create a special, quiet place for listening.

Use such works as "Carnival of the Animals" and "Peter and the Wolf," expanding the children's musical interests and allowing for creative interpretation of the stories told by music.

Encourage children to really listen to music, rather than playing it as "background noise" which is soon ignored.

Games may be played with the instruments. For example, children can close their eyes or turn their backs while another child plays various instruments. The children identify which instrument is making the sound.

Rhythm Sticks

Sand two pieces of doweling, ¾" × 7" long. Paint, add an eye screw on one end of each piece and join with ribbon or braided yarn. Or cut two pieces of ½" × 12" doweling. A few notches cut into the doweling add to the interesting rhythm sounds. Sticks may be painted.

Sound Shakers

Sound shakers may be made from baby food cans or tomato sauce cans. Remove top and bottom portions of can; a stone may be used to smooth any rough edges. The can may be painted or covered for decoration. Cut dowel ¾" × 4" and sand one end. Punch a hole in the side of the can and attach the dowel with a wood screw; a small hole in the center of the dowel end will be helpful. Cut two pieces of used drumheads (contact school music departments) or inner tubes in 4" circles. Punch holes in tube or drumhead 1" apart and ¼" from edge. Place on either end of the can and lace with yarn or string or ribbon. Before closing, insert various objects for different kinds of sounds.

Tambourine, drum beaters, rhythm sticks, rhythm instruments, jingle sticks, stones, coconut shells, shaker bells, sound shaker.

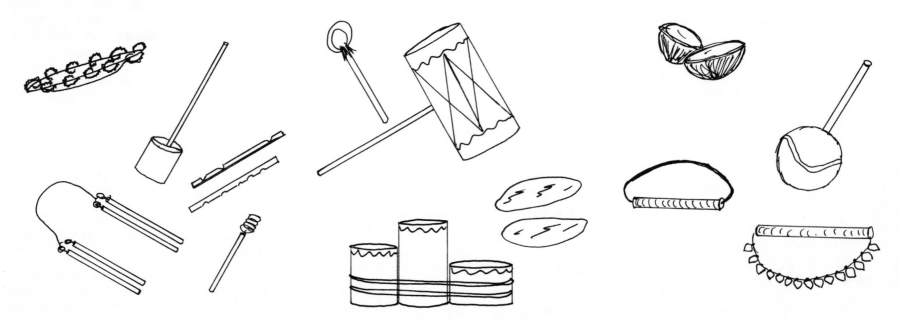

Drums

Drums can be made by taping together three cans or boxes of the same or different sizes. Raffia, yarn, tape, ribbon, string, or plastic lacing; paint; crayons; finger paints; collage; contact paper; and wrapping paper may be used to add to the attractiveness of the drums.

Drum Beaters

Doweling and old tennis balls make good drum beaters. Punch a hole in the ball and push a piece of doweling into the center. Glue the end of doweling that goes into the ball.

Tapping Rhythm Instruments

Two stones, palm size, are useful as tapping rhythm instruments. Stones may be painted and shellacked.

Tambourines

Paste three paper plates together for firmness. Paint or collage with pieces of tissue paper, then shellac. Punch holes about 1" apart and ½" from the rim. Pound bottle tops flat and punch hole near the top of the caps. Tie bottle caps (two together) to the plates with string, yarn, or ribbon and shake—tambourines for dancing.

Jingle Sticks

With old-fashioned clothespins (found in hobby shops), you can make jingle sticks. It is also possible to use doweling or cut pieces of old broom handles. Pound a flat-headed nail through several buttons with large holes into the clothespin, leaving some space so that the buttons can jingle.

Bottle tops can also be used—pound them flat, punch holes into the centers, and attach them to the clothespin like the buttons.

Coconut Shells

Dehusk coconut, saw in half across the grain. Drain fluid: remove and eat the meat. Allow shells to dry thoroughly, then sand edges and outside of shells. Interior may be painted for decoration. Clap together with open ends facing.

Shaker Bells

Indian shaker bells are made with 7" long doweling or broomstick pieces. Cut a coathanger 15" and make a slight arch. String bells on yarn or plastic lacing and wind around the hanger wire. Put an eye screw on each end of the wood; poke each end of the wire through the eye hook and bend back, clamping tight with a pincher. Colorful yarn or ribbons may be added to each end. Hands hold the wooden part for shaking.

Resources

Andrews, P. "Music and Motion: The Rhythmic Language of Children." *Young Children* 32, no. 1 (November 1976): 32-36.

Burnett, M. *Melody, Movement and Language: Teachers Guide of Music in Game Form for Pre-School and Primary Grades.* Saratoga, Calif.: R and E Research Associates, 1973.

Canner, N. *And a Time to Dance.* Boston: Plays, 1975.

Cole, N.R. *Children's Art from Deep Down Inside.* New York: John Day, 1966.

Dimondstein, G. *Children Dance in the Classroom.* New York: Macmillan, 1971.

H'Doubler, M.H. *Dance: A Creative Art Experience.* 2nd ed. Madison, Wisc.: University of Wisconsin Press, 1957.

Hawkinson, J., and Faulhaber, M.F. *Music and Instruments for Children to Make.* Chicago: Albert Whitman, 1969.

Lament, M.M. *Music in Elementary Education: Enjoy, Experience and Learn.* New York: Macmillan, 1976.

Land, L.R., and Vaughan, M.A. *Music in Today's Classroom: Creating, Listening and Performing.* New York: Harcourt Brace Jovanovich, 1973.

Marsh, M.V. *Explore and Discover Music.* New York: Macmillan, 1970.

Mettler, B. *Materials of Dance as a Creative Art Activity.* Tucson, Ariz.: Mettler Studios, 1960.

Peller, L. *The Development of the Child's Self.* New York: Early Childhood Education Council of New York, 1958.

Rowen, B. *Learning Through Movement.* New York: Columbia University Press, 1963.

Russell, J. *Creative Movement in the Primary School.* New York: Frederick A. Praeger, 1968.

Saffran, R.B. *First Book of Creative Rhythms.* New York: Holt, Rinehart and Winston, 1963.

Sheehy, E. D. *Children Discover Music and Dance.* New York: Columbia University Press, 1968.

Stecher, M.B., and McElheny, H. *Music and Movement Improvisation.* Vol. 4. Threshold Early Learning Library. New York: Macmillan, 1972.

Stinson, S.W. "Movement as Creative Interaction with the Child." *Young Children* 32, no. 6 (September 1977): 49-53.

Sewing, knitting, and weaving are challenging for children, offering them pleasure, a sense of accomplishment, and a good bit of pride.

48

Stitchery, Weaving, and Knitting

9

Can you remember the first awkward patch you ever sewed or the first wallet you stitched for your father or mother when you were a child? Can you remember the first scarf you ever knit or the first pot holder or place mat you wove? If you can, you probably can also remember the feelings you had: pleasure, accomplishment, and no doubt a good bit of pride.

Sewing, knitting, and weaving are challenging and worthwhile for children—whether it is using basic stitches to make costumes or butterfly nets, or knitting a whole row without dropping any stitches. Children can create neckties, wall hangings, place mats, puppets, rugs, and scarves with their personal choice of color, shape, texture, and design. They can use these things themselves or proudly give them away as gifts. Children can rub cool smooth satin scraps or velveteen across their cheeks and imagine grandly with scraps of gold or silver braid. Sewing, weaving, and knitting create opportunities for children to be in the warm leisurely company of others of all ages, equally busy with similar projects.

Sewing, knitting, and weaving are excellent activities to develop hand-eye coordination and the precise, accurate use of small muscles as children work to thread the tiny eye of a needle or try to stitch a straight line or thread a leather thong through a pouch. These crafts encourage children to decide on a goal, then figure out what has to be done each step of the way (for example, measuring to see how long a shirt should be, then cutting the material, sewing it together, and hemming it). This is one way children can learn how to plan, solve problems, and figure out how the parts of something go together to make the whole. By measuring an inch of weaving or a yard of material, by using fat and skinny knitting needles or large darning needles and small sewing needles, by saying to themselves, "*Now* I'll cut it out," "*Later* I can put buttons on it," "*After the weekend* I can work on it again," "*One month from now* I can give it to my mother," children can connect real situations and real objects with abstract ideas such as time, length, and size.

As they knit, weave, and sew, children can practice arithmetic operations (for example, subtracting how much of the doll sweater is already knitted from the total length to figure out how many more rows there are to do). Wrestling with pattern and knitting directions gives children excellent practice in reading. They also learn new words by handling and naming materials and equipment: cotton, velvet, oilcloth, cheesecloth, looms, shuttles. Children learn to use language to share ideas, feelings, and information as they work.

Design and beauty are apparent as children decide for themselves why some combinations of color, shape, and texture seem beautiful while others do not, and see that not all people like the same combinations. Children can discover things about the creative arts (for example, the importance of costuming for mood and effect in creative dramatics, puppet shows, and dance). Children can also begin to see the relationships between size, weight, and function (for example, heavy materials make costumes that are hot to wear, darning needles make holes too big for ordinary sewing).

Knitting, sewing, and weaving are useful crafts—the pot holder can be used to pick up the hot pan or take the cookie sheet from the oven. There are opportunities for children to learn craft techniques used by our ancestors and still used by some people today. Elderly people in the community may especially find it meaningful to share their skills with children who are eager to learn new techniques.

In addition, these crafts encourage children to be responsible for their own products and for the care of equipment, tools, and supplies; to see the relationship between safety and responsibility—pins and needles need to be returned to pincushions or proper boxes, scissors should be carried with the points down.

49

Picture frames—to use as looms or for framing pictures stitched on cloth
Scissors and pinking shears
Shuttles—can be made from cardboard
Snaps, hooks and eyes
Spool with tacks for knitting chains of yarn
String, cord, and fine wire
Tape measure
Thimbles
Thread—various colors, #50 and for embroidery
Tracing wheel and paper
Trimmings, bias tape, ribbons, buttons, braid, rickrack
Yarn

Storage

Boxes or drawers for different size materials and supplies, labeled.

Shopping bags, baskets, sewing boxes.

Shoe boxes—cardboard or clear plastic.

Egg cartons or muffin tins for small items, such as hooks and eyes, snaps.

Empty cardboard tubes or spools for winding on ribbons, braid, etc., when not in use.

Patterns and directions for each activity stored with the materials and equipment needed —knitting needles, yarn, and directions together; embroidery hoops, silk, thread, cloth, and stitch patterns together.

Safe place where a child can store a project while still working on it.

TOPICS TO TALK ABOUT WITH CHILDREN

Materials needed—cloth, yarn, scissors, needles (sewing, knitting), hoops—to complete a project.

Sewing, weaving, and knitting create opportunities for children to be in the warm leisurely company of others of all ages, equally busy with similar projects.

Permanent Equipment

Embroidery hoops
Hammer and nails
Knitting needles
Looms—various sizes and shapes
Needles—needles with large holes, large needles for thicker cotton thread and yarn, blunt needles for stitchery
Sewing machine

Learning Materials

Cloth—variety of sizes, shapes, colors, textures, i.e., cotton, flannel, burlap, felt, silk, satin, brocade
Clotheshangers or dowelings for hangings
Dye—various colors
Kapok
Patterns
Pins and pincushions

Sizes, shapes, textures, colors, weights, and various materials.

Sequence in the development of sewing or weaving an item.

Size of needles and thread needed for various activities.

Safety rules about putting needles in pincushions, carrying scissors.

How materials and supplies will be organized and stored when not in use.

Kinds of costumes needed for dramatic play.

How looms are designed and built, new vocabulary of warp and woof.

How stores select clothing for sale.

How dye is made and used.

Handicrafts of ethnic groups.

Proper use of sewing machine.

IDEAS TO TRY

Dye cloth or yarn, make dye colors from vegetables, crepe paper, inks.

Knit a variety of items—scarves, doll sweaters, booties, hats, rugs, ties, belts.

Learn a variety of stitches for hand sewing.

Make original designs and sew costumes.

Make hanks of yarn into balls for looms, yarn dolls and animals, etc.

Make looms of various sizes and shapes; compare resulting products.

Make shuttles for weaving from tongue depressors, cardboard, balsa wood.

Younger children can experience success in making simple items such as pot holders and hand puppets.

Take trips to stores—clothing stores, gift shops, stitchery and yard good shops, sewing factories, 5 and 10 cent stores. Write about and illustrate the experiences.

Make wall hangings using coathangers, cloth, doweling, string. (See Chapter 4.)

Experiment with various cords and yarn for macrame.

Sew curtains, hats, purses, clothing, handkerchiefs, laundry bags, slippers, doll clothing, stuffed animals, pillows.

Sew samplers, Christmas stockings, other holiday gifts.

Sew sit-upons, i.e., oilcloth cover over newspapers, punch holes along outside, and sew together with blunt needles and yarn.

Younger children enjoy burlap and yarn stitchery with large needles.

Sewing hints—Help children learn to use a thimble on the middle finger. Start with simple stitches and add stitches as need and interest are indicated:

1. *Running stitch:* Run the threaded needle in and out of the cloth in a straight or curved line. Take only two or three stitches before pulling the needle through. Stitches and spaces should be even.

2. *Basting stitch:* Same as running stitch except the stitches are larger.

3. *Overcast stitch or whipstitch:* Work from front to back over edge of fabric. This stitch is used to keep edges of seams together and to keep material from raveling.

Sewing, knitting, and weaving are excellent activities to develop hand-eye coordination and the precise, accurate use of small muscles.

4. *Backstitch:* Gives the effect of machine stitching but is done by hand. Take one stitch backward. Bring the needle up through the material a stitch ahead of where you started. Take another backstitch meeting the last stitch and once more bring the needle up through the material a stitch ahead of where you started. A combination of backstitch and running stitch can be used when there is a large area to cover. Take two or three backstitches and then two or more running stitches.

5. *Slip stitch:* Usually used for hemming. Stitches are fine and should not show through on the right side. Pick up two or three threads of material with the threaded needle, then insert needle into the edge of the folded hem and pull the needle through. Continue alternating in this manner, being sure that all the stitches are the same size and the same width apart.

Beanbags—Cut two pieces of felt, heavy ticking, or other tightly woven material. Shapes may be round, square, oblong, shaped like turtles, owls, penguins, etc. Sew together, leaving opening at one end. Turn inside out; pour beans or rice through a funnel into the opening; sew; decorate.

Beanbags

Hat—To make a hat in a hurry in cold weather:

1. Use rectangular piece of fabric or newspaper.

2. Fold in half from top to bottom.

3. Turn corners into center about 2½ inches above bottom of hat.

4. Fold bottom edges up on both sides of hat as you would a cuff. String can be attached for a snug fit.

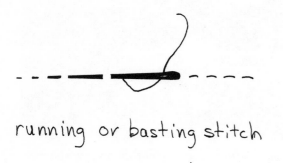

running or basting stitch

backstitch

overcast stitch

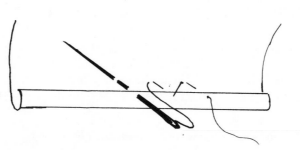

slip stitch

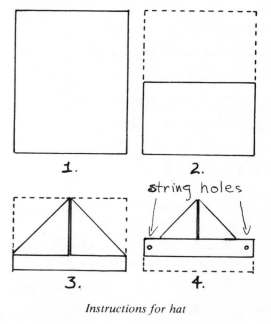

Instructions for hat

Other projects—Try weaving, cloth, basket, or paper; patchwork quilting; appliqué, stuffed dolls, pillows, or animals; needlepoint; rug hooking; crochet; macrame.

Sewing stitches

Resources

Arts and Activities. Journal of Art Education. (Articles on sewing, stitchery, sewing by hand or machine.) September 1967, October 1967, November 1967, May 1968.

Bits and Pieces—Imaginative Uses for Children's Learning. Washington, D.C.: Association for Childhood Education International, 1967.

Enthoven, J. *Stitchery for Children.* Cincinnati, Ohio: Van Nostrand Reinhold, 1967.

Green, S. *Patchwork for Beginners.* New York: Watson-Guptill, 1973.

Ickis, M., ed. *Handicrafts and Hobbies.* New York: Greystone, 1948.

Kroncke, G. *Simple Weaving: Designs, Material, Technique.* Cincinnati, Ohio: Van Nostrand Reinhold, 1973.

LaBarge, L. *Do Your Own Thing with Macrame.* New York: Watson-Guptill, 1973.

Lightbody, D. *Easy Weaving.* New York: Lothrop, Lee & Shepard, 1974.

Linderman, E.W., and Linderman, M.M. *Crafts for the Classroom.* New York: Macmillan, 1977.

Marthamm, A. *Simple Weaving.* New York: Taplinger, 1969.

Miller, I.P., and Lubell, W. *The Stitchery Book: Embroidery for Beginners.* Garden City, N.Y.: Doubleday, 1965.

Rosenberg, S., and Wiener, J. *The Illustrated Hassle-Free Make Your Own Clothes Book.* San Francisco: Straight Arrow, 1971.

Rush, B. *The Stitchery Idea Book.* Cincinnati, Ohio: Van Nostrand Reinhold, 1974.

Short, E. *Introducing Macrame.* New York: Watson-Guptill, 1973.

Grasp the hammer near the end of the handle, not close to the head.
Hit the nail sharply.

54

Working with Wood

10

Have you ever noticed children working with hammers and saws—pounding or sawing away? Their faces are flushed, their clothing is damp, until the nail is finally in or the wood is finally separated into two pieces. By learning to use real tools and methods, school-age children can build things that are impressive and useful—everything from airplanes, wagons, and puppet theaters to elaborate wood sculptures.

They can create, imagine, invent, and decorate. As they cut with saws, pry out nails with a hammer, open the jaws of a wrench, or adjust a vise, children can discover many things. They can find out that lumber is cut from trees, that houses and furniture and stairs and boxes are made by real people, that objects do not ordinarily stand up or stick together but must be arranged to balance and be joined by nails or glue. Working with wood helps children feel a kinship with adult builders and carpenters who also work with wood.

By lugging heavy boards, shaping balsa wood into airplanes and tossing them lightly to the wind, tracing the grain of a plank, and smoothing away splinters and rough edges, children can apply such abstract concepts as weight, size, length, texture, color, and variety to objects from their own world. Children can see the results and importance of mathematical operations such as addition, subtraction, and reversibility—a carefully measured and cut lid really fits its box.

Woodworking develops hand-eye coordination and large and small muscles. As they work, children find it easy to talk with other children about tools, to share ideas, projects, and materials, and to discuss what they are learning to do. Older children may find that younger children appreciate their assistance as they learn new skills. This kind of conversation and cooperation generates good feelings. Woodworking presents problems to be solved, it demands stick-to-it-iveness, and it requires that safety precautions and responsibility for tools be recognized. Working with wood also encourages children to develop good work habits as they plan how to carry out projects and cooperate with other children. What marvelous opportunities for growth woodworking offers to children!

Permanent Equipment

All tools should be real, adult, good quality tools, not toys.

Awl
Brace (drill) and wood bits—6-8″ sweep
C-clamps
File
Hammers—11 to 13 oz., bent claw with drop-forged heads
Knife—utility
Plane
Pliers
Rasp—medium bite, 10″ long
Safety blocks
Sawhorses
Saws—coping (6″ blades), cross-cut (16-20″, good steel), keyhole, rip
Scissors
Screwdrivers—regular and Phillips, short, heavy handled
T-square
Tape measure
Tin snips
Vise
Work bench or table
Wrench—adjustable

Learning Materials

Aprons with pockets
Glue
Graph paper
Hole punch

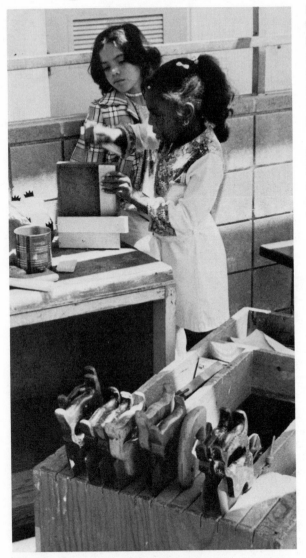

By learning to use real tools and methods, school-age children can build everything from airplanes, wagons, and puppet theaters to elaborate wood sculptures.

Leather pieces
Magnets
Nails with large heads
Paint—water based
Paint brushes
Rags
Ruler
Sandpaper—#1 to #00, wrap around a
   small block
Screws—wood, flat and round heads
Screw eyes and hooks
Shellac
String
Tacks
Turpentine
Varnish
Washers
Wire
Wood—soft pine, poplar, plywood, balsa,
   doweling
Yardstick

Storage

Barrels, boxes, garbage cans, or wastepaper baskets for wood and other materials.

Muffin tins, small plastic containers, or shoe boxes for nails, screws, tacks, etc.

Tools should be hung whenever possible to avoid damage. Pegboards marked with the location of each tool are best. Small items such as clamps can be stored in boxes or drawers. All storage should be labeled and located in the woodworking area.

TOPICS TO TALK ABOUT WITH CHILDREN

How to use each tool, including safety precautions. A first aid kit should be readily available.

How to care for tools—tools should be hung in a dry place, saws sharpened regularly, hammer handles checked for cracks.

How to combine materials such as wood and nails or wood and glue.

Why sandpapering items is sometimes necessary for painting readiness or for safety.

Ideas to enable easier movement—add wheels to a box.

The process of making lumber from trees.

Pulling out nails so they won't bend; use a small block of wood under the hammerhead.

Hammer holding—grasp hammer near the end of the handle, not close to the head. Hit nail sharply.

Planes are used for smoothing and scraping wood. Hold plane with knob forward, push forward with the grain of the wood, holding one hand on knob, the other on the handle. Wood should be firmly clamped to table or workbench.

Children should use a coping saw with even, vertical strokes and without too much pressure. To cut a circle, drill a hole at some point of the circle, remove one end of blade from the saw, pass the blade through the drilled hole. Reclamp blade in frame and saw.

IDEAS TO TRY

Children can design and build games—beanbag stand, ring toss stand, floor checkerboard.

Older children may wish to design and build equipment for dramatic play—stove, refrigerator, sink, shelves.

Wood marionettes are a special challenge.

Design and build a puppet theater; coordinate project with puppet makers, playwrights, and set designers.

Accessory materials can be constructed for block play.

Wood boxes could be made for special uses—toys, blocks, cubbies.

A box with wheels can be hooked to a wagon, trike, or bike.

Build simple bookcases for storage.

Table dollhouses can be made from boxes; simple dollhouse furniture can also be constructed.

Use children's skills to repair equipment—sandpaper rough blocks, pound in nails, glue and clamp a broken drawer.

Sandpaper, paint, and decorate completed items.

Discuss trips taken and career possibilities. Take trips to cabinet shops, lumber mills, furniture factories and stores, paint shops, hardware stores, building being constructed. Invite others in the community to assist children as they work.

Racing Boats

Wood scraps	Paint and/or varnish
Popsicle sticks	Sandpaper
Rubber bands	Graph paper, rulers, compasses, etc.

Adults or older children can explain the basic design and discuss the way in which the boat works. The children can then create a pattern for their boat on graph paper and decide which wood pieces and tools they will need. Individually labeled boxes for storing unfinished projects will be necessary as construction may take several days.

**Topics for exploration
and experimentation with racing boats:**

Will use of thinner or thicker wood affect speed?

Will size of boat affect performance?

Are there ways of improving the initial design?

What is the relation of the design and dynamics of the toy boat to the paddlewheel boats widely utilized in the nineteenth century?

A water table, wading pool, or galvanized tub may be used for racing the boats. Each boat is propelled by twisting stick and rubber bands until taut and then releasing in water. Children may wish to record individual boat performances with a stopwatch. Boat performances can then be compared on a bar graph.

By participating in this activity, children are creating and executing their own designs, hypothesizing about and recording results of data about boats, and experimenting with concepts of propulsion, speed, and design.

Older children may find that younger children appreciate their assistance as they learn new skills. This kind of conversation and cooperation generates good feelings.

Resources

Alton, W. G. *Wooden Toys That You Can Make.* New York: Taplinger, 1972.

Bits and Pieces—Imaginative Uses for Children's Learning. Washington, D.C.: Association for Childhood Education International, 1967.

Brandhofer, M. "Carpentry for Young Children." *Young Children* 27, no. 1 (October 1971): 17-23.

D'Amato, J., and D'Amato, A. *Cardboard Carpentry.* New York: Lion Press, 1966.

Mayesky, M., et al. *Creative Activities for Young Children.* Albany, N.Y.: Delmar, 1975.

Moffitt, M. "Woodworking for Children." New York: Early Childhood Education Council of New York, 1968.

Pitcher, E.G., et al. *Helping Young Children Learn.* 2nd ed. Columbus, Ohio: Charles E. Merrill, 1967.

Rudolph, M., and Cohen, D.H. "The Many Purposes of Blockbuilding and Woodworking." *Young Children* 20, no. 1 (October 1964): 40-46.

Schutz, W.E. *Wooden Toys and Games You Can Make Yourself.* New York: Macmillan, 1975.

Shea, J.G. *Woodworking for Everybody.* 4th rev. ed. Cincinnati, Ohio: Van Nostrand Reinhold 1970.

Weiss, H. *Model Cars and Trucks and How to Build Them.* New York: Thomas Y. Crowell, 1974.

Water, Sand, and Mud

11

"That's really great," you may think as you watch a child painstakingly pour water through a funnel into a bottle or carefully suds and rinse a doll. On the other hand, you may say, "What a mess," as two children gleefully splash in a puddle or pack wet sand on their legs.

Water is a source of pleasure; it feels and usually looks and sounds good—cool and refreshing, smooth and soapy, warm and relaxing. It is a natural material without uses that have been predetermined by a manufacturer. A child's imagination can change water into almost anything—paint, coffee, fire-extinguishing fluid, cakes, chocolate, the ocean. This opens wide the door to the joy of discovery. It creates opportunities for many kinds of play, including messy play with sand and mud which are such fun and so important for children. At the same time, water alone and water combined with sand and mud are materials children of all ages can use. They are not products which must fit someone else's standards.

Children can learn a great deal from working and playing with water and observing how it looks and what it can do. Using water, children can do the things adults do—such as cooking, washing, mixing paints. They can be firefighters, plumbers, or painters for the moment and develop kinship with the adults in the community who actually do these jobs.

As children play with water, sand, and mud, they can find out about absorption, evaporation, floating, freezing, melting, dissolving. They build language skills by adding these and other relevant words (such as *wading, sprinkling, stirring, faucet, spigot, siphon*) to their vocabularies. Through measuring, pouring, hauling, running through, building dams for, and swimming in water, children can sharpen hand-eye coordination and develop both large and small muscles. Cleanup and toileting routines, fisk-tank cleaning, animal feeding, and plant-growing projects can teach children about personal hygiene, their own physical needs, and the physical needs of other living things. Children can also learn about safety firsthand—staying out of deep water when swimming, taking turns in the sprinkler. In each of these water activities, observation, organization, problem solving, mastery of skills, and responsibility for protecting, caring for, and preserving materials are important. In all of these ways children learn to better understand themselves and the world around them.

Careful conservation of water is now a necessity, and in some areas water play activities may have to be curtailed if community supplies are low. To eliminate wasteful uses of water, provide basins or tubs for water play—eliminate the use of running water. Unless water is soapy, it can be used to water plants either indoors or out once it is no longer suitable for play. Soapy water might be used to wash riding toys, to clean doll clothes, or to scrub the sidewalk. Just as children can be creative in using water they can be creative in conserving this precious natural resource.

Permanent Equipment

Aprons
Aquarium
Basins, tubs, pails
Bubble pipes
Cylinders—graduated sizes, metric markings
Garden hose pieces
Kitchen utensils—eggbeaters, sieves, measuring cups, pitchers, baster, muffin tins, funnels, spray bottles
Plastic bottles—various sizes and shapes
Sandbox

Learning Materials

Boats	Rags
Brushes	Straws
Food coloring	

60   *Water, sand, and mud are materials children of all ages can use. They are not products which must fit someone else's standards.*

Storage

Barrels, boxes, or baskets for small items, near place where they will be used.

Sheds for outdoor equipment.

Plastic bags can be used for small water toys.

Chicken wire over the sandbox will discourage cats.

TOPICS TO TALK ABOUT WITH CHILDREN

How water sustains life—of people, pets, wild animals, birds, plants, trees.

Occupations related to water—firefighting, farming, plumbing, fishing, carwashing, street cleaning, lifeguarding, window washing, engineering, resource management, utilities.

Visit the beach, lakes, rivers; a fish hatchery, dam, marina; fire station; car wash. Discuss how water affects our lives. Children may wish to write stories.

Children can experiment with many forms of water—icicles, ice cubes, Popsicles, snow, steam, dew, hail, rain, frost; how water expands when it freezes, mixes with some things but not with others, has air in it, can be absorbed, can change in form.

Why some things sink in water and others float. Why does a nail sink but an oceanliner float?

Explore dams and their functions.

Exercise water safety. All swimming activities should be carefully supervised. What should children know if they are on a boat?

Try new words—*erosion, displacement, absorption, porosity, saturation.*

Older children may wish to pursue water management in their area. Who is responsible? Where are reserves stored?

As children become aware of the relationship between rain, water storage, commercial and personal use, they can begin to explore new ways to conserve water. How much water does it take to flush a toilet? To take a shower? To fill the wading pool? What water uses should be considered essential?

Explore alternate sources of water. How feasible is it to rely on ocean water?

Investigate how pollution affects the water supply and plants and animals confronted with pollution. What happens as the result of an oil spill? If industry dumps hot water into a river?

All children will need to keep a change of clothes at the center. If swimming is available, they will also need their own swimming suits. Check with local health regulations before the excursion.

Careful conservation of water is now a necessity. Soapy water might be used to wash riding toys, to clean doll clothes, or to scrub the sidewalk.

IDEAS TO TRY

Bathe dolls, wash doll clothes, hang wash out to dry.

Wash playhouse furniture, windows; mop playhouse floor.

Children can assist with laundry—towels, washcloths, cot sheets, rags.

Water plants, lawn, and garden.

Clean fishbowls, aquarium, pet cages.

Carry pails of water to sandbox or mudhole.

Build dams and bridges.

Wash paintbrushes, tables, easels, painting aprons.

Mix easel paint, dough, clay, finger paint.

Wash seashells, stones.

Float cork, feathers, balsa wood, leaves, small boats.

Blow soap bubbles.

Splash in wading pool; swim in community pool.

Experiment with water temperature; study water through sunlight; observe reflection in water puddles; observe what happens to water squirted on warm cement; watch air bubbles rise to top of water in a full jar of water; watch what happens when a jar of water covered with a lid is placed outside in winter weather; watch snow melt when brought into a warm room, watch what happens to the waterline when you put a stone, sponge, or piece of cloth in a measuring cup of water; watch which things mix and which do not mix with water—oil, salt, syrup, sugar, baking soda.

Fill glasses with different amounts of water (color with food coloring if desired) and play melodies.

Sandbox

Encourage children to experiment with sand. When does it pour easily? When can it be molded? What happens if water is poured on it?

Where does sand come from? How can you find out?

What other minerals are extracted from the earth? How are they used?

Fill muffin tin with water. In three of the sections place three basic colors. Children can use eyedroppers to mix colors.

Explore what happens when mud dries. What different kinds of soil create different types of mud?

Select a site for mud play with the children—where should it be? What considerations should be made?

Encourage children to begin a water conservation campaign. Who can they contact? What can they do?

Sandbox—Five or six tires arranged in a circle can be the basis for an interesting sandbox. The center space and each of the tires can be filled with sand. One tire can be used for water play if cut in half and filled with water.

Waterfalls— Cut milk cartons in half lengthwise. Punch a hole in one side and extend a straw through the hole. Build various levels in the sandbox; arrange the cartons so that the water drops from one carton to the next, forming a waterfall.

Walnut shell boat—Partly fill half a walnut shell with melted wax. When wax is set, pierce a 1″ × ½″ paper sail with a toothpick and stick the toothpick into the wax.

Origami paper boats are fun to fold. What kinds of paper work best?

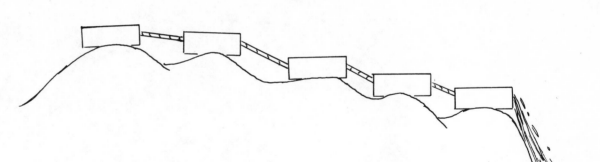

Milk carton waterfall

Balsa wood sailboat

Balsa wood	Rubber bands
¼″ dowel stick	Saws
Glue	Ruler
Sheets	Tubs for dye
Dye	¼″ brace (drill) and bit

Children cut balsa wood into boat shapes of their own design. With a ¼″ bit, drill a hole into the wooden hull but not through it. Cut a length of dowel stick, taking care not to make it too long. (This raises the boat's center of gravity and it will tip over easier.) Glue dowel into the hole. To make a sail, cut sheets into squares, gather fabric randomly and wrap tightly with rubber bands. Dip sails into tubs of hot fabric dye. After sails have dried, attach to crossbars (Popsicle sticks work well) and attach crossbars to dowel mast with nails.

Resources

Althouse, R., and Main, C. *Science Experiences for Young Children.* New York: Teachers College Press, 1975.

Guillaume, J. "Water, Water, Everywhere." *Parents' Magazine,* August 1959.

Harlan, J.D. *Science Experiences for the Early Childhood Years.* New York: Macmillan, 1976.

Harris, D. "The Wonderful World of Water Play." *P.T.A. Magazine,* June 1967.

Hartley, R.E., et al. *Understanding Children's Play.* New York: Columbia University Press, 1952.

Hill, D. M. *Mud, Sand, and Water.* Washington, D.C.: National Association for the Education of Young Children, 1977.

Holt, B. *Science with Young Children.* Washington, D.C.: National Association for the Education of Young Children, 1977.

Leeper, D., et al. *Good Schools for Young Children.* 3rd ed. New York: Macmillan, 1969.

Levens, D. "A Sink with Running Water." *Journal of Nursery Education* 14, no. 3 (Spring 1959): 24.

Lowenfeld, M. *Play in Childhood.* New York: John Wiley & Sons, 1967.

West, S. "A Sense of Wonder—Parents and Children Together." *Young Children* 29, no. 6 (September 1974): 363-368.

Cooking

12

Preparing food—and the menu-planning, shopping, setting the table, serving, eating, and cleanup that go with it—gives children wonderful opportunities to use all five senses: to see the beauty of color, shape, and arrangement; to smell everything from apple pie to boiled cabbage; to taste salty, sour, sweet, bitter, bland foods and spices; to touch warm, soft bread dough, slippery fish, rough coconuts; to hear popcorn popping, water boiling, pancakes frying.

At the same time, opportunities for delicious anticipation arise while the cake is baking, the ice cream is freezing, or the gelatin is setting, topped off by the physical pleasure of eating the finished product. Sometimes this pleasure may be increased by opportunities to find a favorite eating spot inside in a box or corner, or outside rooms and yards into more open settings such as parks and recreation areas for picnics. Cooking gives children the opportunity to use what they have learned, to do some of the things adults do, and to turn out products that can be appreciated, admired, eaten, shared, or given as gifts. Cooking also gives the child a chance to be away from the larger group, and sometimes to be alone with an adult or child, working almost as if they were at home.

There are opportunities to develop hand-eye coordination in such activities as shelling peas, sorting vegetables, and decorating cookies, as well as opportunities to develop large and small muscles by cranking the ice cream freezer, pushing the shopping cart, rolling dough, mashing potatoes, and sifting the flour. There are opportunities to solve problems and see the effects of attempted solutions—what to do when something sticks to a pan, when the dough does not rise, when liquids are too hot, when something might spoil. There are opportunities to find out more about such things as:

Time—the length of one hour, five minutes, one minute; how long it takes to bake bread or boil an egg.

Changes in matter—gelatin changing to a solid in the refrigerator and liquid in the sun; egg whites expanding and thickening when beaten.

Number—counting change at the market; napkins and cups necessary for lunch or snack; number of eggs, tablespoons of shortening, cups of flour; computing cost per serving.

Quantity—measuring cups and pints and quarts, dividing recipes in half, estimating number of servings.

Classification and grouping—carrots, peas, beans are vegetables; water, milk, vanilla extract are liquids.

Cooking gives children many opportunities to read and write as they work with recipes, adapt quantities, and follow directions. It helps them to extend vocabularies by using and naming such objects as graters, strainers, and sieves, and processes such as fold, whip, and simmer. Planning menus, picnics, and parties, gives children more opportunities to develop language skills as well as to learn how to work with other children and adults.

Cooking provides the perfect vehicle for helping children learn about nutrition and health. Planning for snacks and meals can be done with the children—selecting dairy products, fresh fruits and vegetables, meats, and whole grains, rather than sweets, processed foods, and items with little or no nutritional value. A garden at the center (see Chapter 13) can be an additional stimulus to interest in fresh produce.

Along with a balanced diet goes the proper care of food—washing fresh fruits and vegetables, refrigerating items which spoil easily, cooking with small amounts of water to preserve vitamins and minerals. A good source of free information on nutrition and preparation is your local cooperative extension service.

By eating foods from many cultures and learning about the traditions that go with them, children can learn about other people, or perhaps they can share part of their family's world with friends and teachers. They can also learn that different ethnic foods are not bad or strange but can be fun, delicious, and interesting.

Cooking also helps children learn that safety is no accident. Turning pan handles away from the outside of the stove and using pot holders to take things out of the oven are just two safety measures cooks employ.

Cooking offers almost limitless opportunities for learning and sharing. What new ideas would the children in your center like to try?

Permanent Equipment

Bottle opener
Bowls
Cake pans
Can opener
Colander
Cookie cutters
Cookie sheets
Cutting boards
Eggbeater
First aid kit
Fork—long-handled
Grater—hand, four-sided
Knives—paring
Measuring spoons and cups
Pancake turner
Pitchers
Refrigerator
Rolling pin
Saucepans
Scrapers—rubber
Sifter
Skillet—heavy
Spatulas
Spoons—wooden, slotted
Stove
Strainers
Vegetable brushes
Vegetable peeler

Add if possible:

Apple corer
Blender
Candy thermometer
Cheese slicer
Clock or timer
Corn popper
Egg slicer
Electric frying pan
Electric mixer
Gelatin molds
Hot plate—two-burner, adjustable heat
Ice cream freezer
Meat grinder
Muffin tins
Orange juicer—hand squeezing
Pastry brushes
Portable bake oven
Potato masher
Tongs

Storage

Labeled boxes, shelves, baskets, and cabinets, nesting materials when possible.

Plastic bags, closed containers.

Knives kept separate from other utensils.

Storage should be located near appliances.

TOPICS TO TALK ABOUT WITH CHILDREN

Sequence of how things are grown, harvested, packaged, transported, placed in stores and markets, sold, transported to homes, cooked, served.

The nutritional value of different foods, and why good nutrition is vital to health.

Preparation of foods—washing, cooking, serving.

Foods which can be eaten raw—spinach, lettuce, fruits—but can also be used in a variety of different ways—creamed spinach, lettuce in salads, fruits in gelatin, pies, cookies, or cakes.

Safety factors—turning pot handles back from the front of the stove, mopping up spills immediately, cutting safely away from body, using pot holders, not bending faces over steaming pots, using a cutting board.

Changes which take place when foods are chilled or heated—gelatin, popcorn, rice, macaroni, split peas.

The difference in the taste and texture of different foods—sweet orange, sour lemon, soft bread, crunchy toast, spicy enchiladas, mild tapioca pudding.

Names, colors, and textures of different foods —apples, cucumbers, peppers, bananas, green beans, peas, squash.

The economics of purchasing food in markets, neighborhood stores, delicatessens, roadside stands.

How to determine quality, quantity, weight, size, price.

The people who grow, process, package, and sell foods.

Holiday and ethnic foods.

Preparing and serving well-balanced meals.

Indoor and outdoor cooking.

Formulate plans with children for shopping, preparation, serving, and cleanup. Discuss how weather affects food supplies. What role does agriculture play in the economy?

Alternatives to traditional food and nutritional food sources.

IDEAS TO TRY

Take trips to a neighborhood market, fish market, bakery, delicatessen, vegetable farm, orchard, cannery, dairy, meat processing plant. Discuss and record the experiences.

Children can plan menus, prepare shopping lists, and shop. Encourage parents to include children in these activities at home.

Use mechanical equipment—eggbeater, ice cream freezer, blender, scale, electric frying pan, portable bake oven, corn popper. Discuss what makes them work.

Shell peas, prepare green beans, scrape carrots, squeeze lemons and oranges for juice.

Shake containers of cream to make butter, add salt or eat on saltines.

Make gelatin, applesauce, vegetable soup.

Bake bread, biscuits, muffins, popovers, gingerbread people, yeast bread and rolls, pizza.

Toast sandwiches, make cinnamon toast, fry pancakes and potatoes.

Make sandwiches for a picnic lunch.

Pop corn, grate coconut, shred lettuce.

Blend milk and juices for milkshakes.

Roast hot dogs, ears of corn, potatoes, ranchburgers, hamburgers, kabobs on sticks, bread and buns over charcoal; toast marshmallows.

Make desserts—ice cream, puddings, cakes, cookies, pies, custards.

Plan and prepare snacks—stuff celery; cut up cauliflower, beets, and turnips; serve different shaped crackers and sandwiches.

Children can write a cookbook or prepare a recipe file including favorite recipes as well as those continuously used. Include parents' favorites.

Devil, hardcook, fry, scramble, and poach eggs.

Snack ideas for children to prepare

Ants on a log (recipe p. 68)
Apple wedges
Applesauce (recipe p. 67)
Bananas—sliced or frozen
Bean sprout sandwiches
Bread (recipe p. 68)
Cabbage leaves
Carrot sticks
Carrot sticks with olives on ends
Celery sticks—stuffed with cream cheese or peanut butter
Cheese with pretzels or crackers
Cinnamon toast—painted (recipe p. 68)
Cookies; paintbrush cookies (recipe p. 68)
Crackers—assorted, spread with cream cheese or peanut butter
Cupcake ice cream cones (recipe p. 68)
Cupcakes—decorated
Donuts—easy (recipe p. 68)
Frozen fruit treats (recipe p. 67)
Fruit gelatin
Funnel cakes (recipe p. 68)
Granola—homemade
Green pepper slices
Ice cream
Melon chunks

Muffins
Nuts—assorted
Orange wedges
Peanut butter balls (recipe p. 67)
Pigs in blankets (recipe p. 68)
Popcorn
Puddings
Pudding-wiches (recipe p. 68)
Pumpkin seeds—baked
Toast—spread with peanut butter, cheese, or honey
Tomato wedges

Applesauce

Cut apples in quarters, leaving skins on. Add ½″ of water to pot; bring to boil. Cover and cook slowly for 20-30 minutes or until soft. Add sugar if needed. Force through sieve. Serve warm or cold. (Changes in color, texture, and form which are vividly demonstrated in this procedure are a delight for children to observe.)

Frozen fruit treats

Cut fruit in half, squeeze enough juice to fill ice cube tray. Add sugar or honey if needed. When partially frozen, insert stick upright into each section of tray and let freeze.

Peanut butter balls

½ cup peanut butter	Raisins
2 cups powdered milk	Whole grain cereal
2 tablespoons honey	Coconut

Mix peanut butter, powdered milk, and honey. Add raisins if desired. Roll in balls, then roll balls in cereal or coconut. Chill.

Pigs in blankets

Bread slices   Cheese slices
Hot dogs   Toothpicks

Place cheese and hot dog on bread. Roll two ends of bread up around hot dog and secure with toothpick. Bake in preheated oven until hot (350° for 20 minutes).

Bread

1 cup lukewarm water   2 tablespoons sugar
1 cake of yeast   2 cups flour
2 tablespoons   1 teaspoon salt
   shortening

Add yeast to water and stir until yeast melts. Add shortening and sugar; stir. Then add flour. Be sure dough is very stiff. Set in warm place until dough doubles in size (about 1 hour). Add salt. Shape into 8 rolls; set in warm place until rolls double in size again (about 1 hour). Bake about 15 minutes at 450° F (230° C).

Ants on a log

Celery   Raisins
Peanut butter

Separate and wash celery stalks. Fill each stalk with peanut butter. Place raisins in a row on top of the peanut butter.

Cupcake ice cream cones

Cake batter   Cup-style ice cream
     cones

Mix cake batter according to directions. Pour into ice cream cones until ¾ full. Bake according to directions for cupcakes. A scoop of ice cream on top makes this an extra special treat for parties.

Painted cinnamon toast

Bread   Cinnamon
Milk   Sugar
Food coloring   Butter

Mix "paint" by combining food coloring with milk. Paint designs or pictures on one side of the bread with small clean paintbrushes. Place bread, painted side up, under broiler and toast. While bread is still hot, spread with butter and sprinkle with cinnamon and sugar.

Paintbrush cookies

Sugar cookie dough   Egg yolk paint

Roll out any recipe of sugar cookie dough. Cut out designs and place on a greased cookie sheet. With small, clean paintbrushes, draw designs with egg yolk paint.

Egg yolk paint—Blend one egg yolk with ¼ teaspoon water. Divide into 2 or 3 small cups and add a different food coloring to each cup.

Pudding-wiches

1½ cups milk   1 package instant pud-
½ cup peanut butter   ding, any flavor
     24 graham crackers

Add milk slowly to peanut butter in a deep, narrow bottom bowl. Blend until smooth. Add pudding mix; beat slowly until well mixed (about 2 minutes). Let stand 5 minutes. Spread filling about ½" thick on 12 graham crackers; top with remaining crackers. Freeze until firm (about 3 hours). Makes 12.

Funnel cakes

Pancake batter   Syrup
Butter

After mixing the pancake batter, fill meat basters with the batter or pour it through a funnel onto a hot griddle, making shapes, letters, or designs. Cook as any pancake.

Easy donuts

Refrigerator-style bak-   Powdered sugar,
   ing powder biscuits   cinnamon sugar,
Cooking oil   or chocolate

Mold each biscuit into any shape desired. Drop the molded donut into hot fat and fry until golden and puffy. Roll the donut in powdered sugar, cinnamon sugar, or chocolate, and eat.

Cook's hat

A circle of material about 12" in diameter can be gathered with large basting stitches. Sew headband to the gathered edge. The cook's hat can also be made from newspaper for a onetime use.

Cook's hat

Cooking aprons

Children can make their own aprons from windowshade material or lightweight oilcloth. Fabric should be folded in half and pattern marked to fit the child. Cut with pinking shears. If desired, edges can be turned and stitched. Use colorful yarn to tie at the waist.

Cook's apron

Resources

Berger, E., et al. "Mommy, Would You Come into the Kitchen Please?" Sacramento, Calif.: California Children's Lobby, 1973.

Carmichael, V. *Science Experiences for Young Children.* Los Angeles: Southern California Association for the Education of Young Children, 1969.

Cobb, V. *Arts and Crafts You Can Eat.* Philadelphia: J.B. Lippincott, 1974.

Cobb, V. *Science Experiments You Can Eat.* Philadelphia: J.B. Lippincott, 1972.

Cole, A., et al. *A Pumpkin in a Pear Tree: Creative Ideas for Twelve Months of Holiday Fun.* Boston: Little, Brown, 1976.

Cooking and Eating with Children—A Way to Learn. Washington, D.C.: Association for Childhood Education International, 1974.

Croft, K. *The Good for Me Cook Book.* Saratoga, Calif.: R and E Research Associates, 1971.

Engel, R.C. "Popping Corn." *Young Children* 20, no. 3 (January 1965): 186-187.

Ferreira, N. *The Mother-Child Cook Book.* Menlo Park, Calif.: Pacific Coast Publishing Co., 1969.

Ferreira, N. "Teachers' Guide to Educational Cooking in the Nursery School—An Everyday Affair." *Young Children* 29, no. 1 (November 1973): 23-32.

Galen, H. "Cooking in the Curricula." *Young Children* 32, no. 2 (January 1977): 59-68.

Johnson, G., and Povey, G. *Metric Milk Shake and Witches Cakes.* New York: Citation Press, 1976.

Kohn, B. *Easy Gourmet Cooking for Young People and Beginners.* New York: Bobbs-Merrill, 1973.

Kositsky, V. "What in the World Is Cooking in Class Today? Multiethnic Recipes for Young Children." *Young Children* 33, no. 1 (November 1977): 23-31.

Kositsky, V., McFarlane, B., and Swenson, M. *I Made It Myself Cookbook.* Berkeley, Calif.: Merritt, 1973.

Levine, L. *Kids in the Kitchen Cookbook.* New York: Macmillan, 1973.

Martel, J., ed. *Smashed Potatoes: A Kid's Eye View of the Kitchen.* Boston: Houghton Mifflin, 1974.

Paul, A., and Hawkins, A. *Kids Cooking.* New York: Archway, 1971.

Peppiatt, M. *The Cooking with Kids Cookbook.* Los Angeles: Price, Stern, Sloan, 1969.

Pinkwater, J. *The Natural Snack Cookbook: 151 Good Things to Eat.* New York: Four Winds Press, 1975.

Pitcher, E. G., et al. *Helping Young Children Learn.* 2nd ed. Columbus, Ohio: Charles E. Merrill, 1967.

Stein, S. *The Kids Kitchen Takeover.* New York: Workman, 1975.

Observing, experimenting, checking in books, and asking adults, children can find answers to many of the questions they have about their surroundings.

70

Science, Nature, and Gardening

13

Children love to learn about the world—light, heat, sound, electricity, animals, plants, earth, space. *Things happen!* Seeds come up, magnets attract, the frog's tongue pops out to eat a bug, snow falls, ice freezes. Observing, experimenting, checking in books, and asking adults, children can find answers to many of the questions they have about their surroundings: Do earthworms have teeth? How do plants absorb water? What is sound? How does a switch turn the light on? Children can also make things happen themselves. For example, they can make an electric current flow when they complete the circuit between a battery and a light.

The world is full of wonderful things to see, hear, smell, taste, and touch—bright autumn leaves, turquoise dragonflies, birds and insects singing, flowers, honey from a honeycomb, warm earth, soft and furry caterpillars.

Children discover many of the basic principles of physics and chemistry by watching what happens as they do various things. They can learn about:

- *Force*—by pushing boxes and pulling wagons.

- *Forms of energy* (and the idea of energy as a force that does work)—by watching as steam makes the teakettle whistle, gasoline makes the car run, sun and water make plants grow, food makes people feel strong, electricity makes the record player run.

- *Sound*—by feeling vibrations on a drum, seeing the vibrations of a tuning fork, twanging a rubber band guitar.

- *Magnetism*—by using magnets to pick up steel or iron but not aluminum, plastic, or wood; by watching two magnets attract or repel each other.

- *Friction*—by seeing roller skates make sparks on bumpy pavement, feeling wood get hot while sandpapering it.

- *Acceleration*—by rolling slowly down from the top of the hill and really whirling by the time they get to the bottom.

- *Chemical reactions* (or lack of them)—by mixing baking soda and vinegar to make a miniature volcano, shaking oil and water together.

Working with seeds, plants, batteries, animals, and insects helps children to look at things carefully and to notice their shape, color, size, weight, texture, action, and behavior. Children learn to think of one experience or discovery *in relationship to another*—"This moth has six legs like the butterfly"; "It rained the last time we had clouds like this, too"—and to notice similarities, differences, changes—"I'm taller than my baby brother but he's growing"; "There aren't any pretty orange leaves in winter."

By making an ant farm like the one in a book they have read, displaying rocks or insects the way the museum did, trying out a suggestion that levers can move heavy objects, children can discover that what they learned from reading or going on field trips or talking in class can be useful and practical. Working with adults who encourage curiosity, children can learn to feel comfortable asking questions and saying, "I don't know," "I don't understand yet," and "How can I find out?" They can learn to figure out their own answers to questions and problems by observing, testing, checking, and reaching conclusions.

Children can become aware of their own growth as they discover they can reach bicycle pedals they could not touch last year and that they need longer pants legs and sweater sleeves and bigger shoes, or as they make a new mark on the "growing chart." They can observe the orderly sequence of life stages—conception, birth, growth, old age, death—repeated over and over again as the hamsters mate and baby hamsters are born, polliwogs grow into frogs, the aged rabbit dies. This helps them see themselves as part of the pattern of the world of living things.

By seeing tiny bugs hiding in grass and under rocks, bees pollinating flowers, rain and sun nourishing plants, large insects eating smaller ones, birds eating insects, animals eating birds—and then considering their own use of trees, water, air, and animals, children can develop a sense of how living and nonliving things depend on each other. They can learn to respect the world of nature and from this respect will grow the desire to learn to protect it as well as enjoy it.

Children can also learn to work together—to use a common bottle to put bugs in, to share the bells and light and wires for the gadget board, to take turns feeding the turtle. They have opportunities to learn words related to their observations and discoveries—erosion, pollination, mutation, adaptability, conservation, pollution, fertilization, reflection, vibration—which will accurately tell what they found out.

Children have opportunities to read and write, pursuing a topic in a science book, writing notebooks about weather, labeling bottles with specimens, writing up a project, making up lists of materials and equipment needed, making signs asking that others not touch their project. They find these skills useful ways for discovering, recording, and communicating. Children also have opportunities to learn how to use equipment such as microscopes, prisms, magnifying glasses, tape recorders, and record players carefully and correctly. They learn to accept the responsibilities of caring for the equipment, animals, gardens, and individual projects.

Permanent Equipment

Aprons
Balance
Binoculars
Camera
Compass
Electric bells
Flashlight
Funnels
Gardening tools
Globe
Gyroscope
Kaleidoscope
Kites
Magnets—various sizes and shapes
Magnifying glass
Maps
Microscope
Mirrors
Musical instruments
Pails
Prisms
Reference books
Scale
Stand magnifier
Stethoscope
Telescope/periscope
Thermometer
Timer
Tire pump
Tongs
Tuning fork

Learning Materials

Adhesive tape
Ant farm
Aquarium
Balloons
Balsa wood
Batteries—dry cell
Birdfeeders
Bird nests
Bulbs, seeds, plants
Cages for classroom pets
Cardboard, cardboard tubes
Cellophane paper
Cork
Crepe paper
Feathers
Felt pens
Fish, toads, frogs, tadpoles
Hardware for gadget boards
Iron filings
Jars, cans, boxes, and milk cartons
Masking tape
Nails, screws
Notebooks
Pinwheels
Plaster of paris
Plunger and other suction gadgets
Rocks, pebbles
Rubber bands
Rubber tubing—pieces
Ruler, tape measure
Salt—coarse
Sand
Sandpaper
Scissors
Seashells
Soda, starch, sugar, salt, vinegar
Soil
Straws
Syringes, squeeze bottles
Terrarium
Vivarium for toads and frogs
Yardstick

Storage

Boxes, cabinets, shelves, baskets, hooks
—label or draw sketches where equipment or material goes.

Special containers for breakable items (as few as possible).

Plastic bags for small articles.

Several small cabinets rather than one large one so children have easy access to materials.

Locked cupboards with containers clearly labeled for chemicals such as alcohol, turpentine, iodine, bleach, glycerine, etc.

TOPICS TO TALK ABOUT WITH CHILDREN

Machines with wheels which help us get from place to place—taxis, bicycles, buses, automobiles, trains, airplanes, motorcycles, wheelchairs.

Other things with wheels which are fun—roller skates, skateboards, merry-go-round, Ferris wheel, scooter, wagon, record player, fishing reel.

Items with wheels which help us in the house and garden—lawn mower, casters on furniture, telephone dial, eggbeater, wheelbarrow.

Magnets—what they attract and what they do not attract; a magnet attracts through paper, glass, and wood.

How vacuum cleaners, blenders, hair dryers, irons, and various other electrical equipment—lamps, refrigerators, waffle irons, percolators, clocks, television sets, hot plates, streetlights, traffic signals—work.

How wall plugs, light sockets, extension cords, and light switches are used.

Energy—food is a source of energy; light energy helps us find our way; wind or water produces electrical energy.

The need for conserving limited fuel resources.

Things which help us in our daily living—needles, scissors, hammers and nails, typewriters, can openers.

How things look through a magnifying glass, a telescope, a periscope, binoculars.

How to use and store garden tools; safety measures.

Composition, color, and texture of soil; different colors of soil—red, black, brown, yellow; different textures—sandy, rocky, hard, soft, clay.

Seeds—soaking before planting; putting bulbs in refrigerator before planting; how seeds travel—wind, birds, fur of animals, clothing, spontaneous shoot out; time to plant seeds and bulbs; the effect of sun, light, and temperature on germination, soil moisture, etc.

Preparation of garden soil—dug, spaded, fertilized; why clods of soil are broken before planting.

Grasses of importance—rice, corn, wheat, rye, barley, oats; where they grow; how seeds are sown; how crops are used.

How and why buds sprout—roots growing down and stems growing up.

Plants—parts of plants and their functions. Plants are living things which grow and reproduce; different kinds of plants live in different environments—some, such as the cactus, require sunlight, others, such as the fern, prefer shade.

Weather—temperature, wind, and humidity. How weather affects our lives.

What can be eaten raw and what must be cooked.

How animals and plants depend on each other.

Identifying things by sight—color, size, shape.

Identifying things by smell—perfume, garlic, toast, burning leaves.

Identifying things by taste—bitter, sweet, salty, sour, crunchy, bland, spicy.

Identifying things by touch—hard, smooth, rough, soft, bumpy, large, small, prickly. Children can create touching boxes or feeling bags.

Identifying things by sound—loud, shrill, squeaky, raspy, whispery.

Children can learn to respect the world of nature, and from this respect will grow the desire to learn to protect it as well as enjoy it.

73

Value of insects, bugs, and spiders, earthworms, snails—how they look and move, what they do, what gardeners should know about them.

Space—how rockets are propelled into space; one's relationship to space.

Household chemicals and how they are used—vinegar, salt, sugar, ammonia, baking soda, washing soda, vegetable dyes, bleaches.

IDEAS TO TRY

Plant an outdoor garden. Prepare the earth, marking seeded areas with signs of what is being grown. Water, weed, harvest, taste, discuss.

Grow carrot, turnip, beet tops, potato, and pineapple in dish of water.

Sprinkle flax, parsley, or bird seed on top of damp sponge placed in a pie pan.

Fill a tray with damp cotton. Put in rows of beet, radish, bean, and lettuce seeds. Keep moist, transplant.

Plant bulbs in small cartons, cans, or paper cups which can be given as gifts.

Grow herbs in an indoor garden. Study seed catalogs for a wide selection.

Collect seed pods. Paint, arrange, and string.

Arrange flowers. Learn their names. Learn functions of pistil, stamen, anther, nectar, blossom, petal, bud.

Make an indoor observation shelf and study the effects of the lack of air, sun, and/or water on plant growth.

Take nature walks and record what was seen and heard. Take care to leave the area just as it was found or better.

Make leaf prints on paper, cardboard, or plaster of paris.

Make a leaf collection. Note similarities and differences in shape, size, color, texture, thickness of leaves. Learn the names of the trees from which the leaves came.

Put some soil in a jar and cover it tightly. Why do drops of moisture gather in the jar?

Put some water in a jar. Drop a stone in and watch how the waterline changes. Drop other materials in and see which ones absorb water.

Press flowers; make wax paper flower and leaf transparencies.

Collect nails, clips, thumbtacks, wire, seeds, buttons, etc., and see which are attracted to magnets.

Make a museum of rocks, shells, nuts, insects, nests, plants, bark, stones, cactus.

Collect different types of rock—pumice, quartz, limestone with shells, mica, coal, lava, rocks with plant imprints.

Make gadget boards with lights, switches, bells, and batteries.

Make touching boxes with things that are rough, soft, bumpy, long, short, round, hard, wet, smooth; use shells, bark, glass, cloth, felt, pine cones, sandpaper, sand, clay, paper, velvet, silk, absorbent cotton, pine needles, leaves, flowers. Have children identify by name and texture.

Collect bells and note differences in sounds.

Play tuning fork or other instruments which make sounds when struck.

Fill glasses with different amounts of water (color with food coloring) and note differences in sounds when struck.

Experiment with matter—bulk, weight, divisibility, porosity, elasticity, impenetrability—by noting differences in size and weight of blocks; weight of child on a scale; sawing wood into two pieces or cutting fruit in half; wiping up spilled milk with a sponge; pouring water into a sandbox; popping corn; cooking rice; stretching rubber bands; trying to hammer nails into very hard wood.

Experiment with measurements—length or height using rulers, tape measures, and yardsticks; volume using cups, pitchers, or other containers for milk or juice; time using a calendar, three-minute glass timer, or clock; weight using a scale; temperature using a thermometer.

Make "Rube Goldberg" machines from odds and ends, pulleys, gears, clocks and watches, things with wheels, and wind-up toys.

Care for, feed, and observe frogs, toads, tadpoles, horned toads, lizards, salamanders, rabbits, guinea pigs, gerbils, hamsters.

Put snails in a jar with air holes in the lid and observe with a magnifying glass.

Make a worm farm using a box or tray filled with soil; add a little cornmeal and keep moist.

Make an ant village in a tray filled with anthill soil, small piece of moist sponge, and sugar; place tray in pan of water.

Fill a jar with seawater; put in some seaweed. Cap tightly so air does not get in and seaweed will last for months if set near light. Shake occasionally so the seaweed is in motion.

Incubate eggs. Observe and care for baby chicks. Be sure you have provision for care of chickens as they grow.

Observe shadows; make shadows. Notice the difference in length of a shadow according to the time of day.

Use air pump to blow up balloons; make paper airplanes; use walnut shell boats (see p. 63) with sails and blow around in a shallow pan.

Collect pictures and make scrapbooks; for example, make a scrapbook of appliances which use electricity—vacuum cleaners, irons, electric stoves, toasters, mixers, blenders, shavers, hot plates, hair dryers, lamps, lawn mowers.

Gardening projects

Friendly egghead—Hardcook an egg; carefully cut off top and hollow out the edible portion and eat. Use a felt pen to draw a design or face on the bottom half of the shell. Staple a strip of stiff paper together to make a supporting base. Fill eggshell with potting soil, then plant grass seed. Keep soil moist.

Potato farming—Put soil into an opaque plastic trash bag until it is almost full. Select a sprouted potato and cut into pieces, making sure that two or more sprouts are in each section. Plant three cuttings in a bag, setting each five inches deep. Leave sack open at the top. Put in a warm, sunny place and keep the soil moist but not soggy. When leaf growth is four or five inches high, save the biggest plant and discard the others. After five or six weeks, gently reach into the soil to see if you can feel the new potatoes.

Sprouts—Buy alfalfa seeds at a health food store —one ounce will yield four or five crops of sprouts. Use two tablespoons for each quart jar you start. Soak seeds overnight; drain well and put in jar. Stretch a piece of cheesecloth over the jar and secure with a rubber band. Set the jar in a warm spot in indirect light. Rinse seeds with water twice a day; drain well after each rinsing. The seeds will sprout in four or five days. Use sprouts in salads or in sandwiches.

Coconut birdfeeder—Saw a quarter out of a coconut and leave some of the meat in. Punch a hole in the top and tie with string. The birds will enjoy a tropical luncheon.

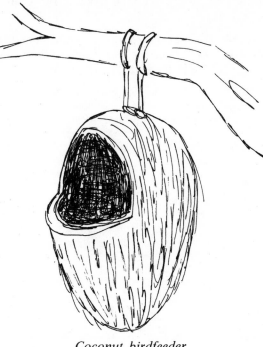

Coconut birdfeeder

Pine cone birdfeeder—Coat pine cone with peanut butter and roll in sunflower seeds.

Wooden birdfeeders or houses—Children may wish to construct wooden birdfeeders or houses. Prior to construction, adults may wish to initiate discussions about birds native to the area and their eating habits; set up a library center with materials about birds as well as methods for observation and identification, including illustrations of birds; encourage children to keep individual observation logs including information on birds sighted (identifiable traits—wings, color, feathers, beaks), choice of feeders, frequency of sightings, time of day, etc. The information can be charted to share with other children.

Children can plan and take trips to various places as they extend their knowledge of science —farms, factories, zoos, ponds, arboretums, botanical gardens, nurseries, museums, airports, etc.

Explore careers in science with children. Help them discover occupations which may be new to them—forester, fisheries and wildlife management, medical researcher, food chemist, engineer, etc.

Stimulate new and creative ways of thinking about the world—how different it will be when the children have grown up!

Resources

Althouse, R., and Main, C. *Science Experiences for Young Children.* New York: Teachers College Press, 1975.

Anderson, R., et al. *Developing Children's Thinking Through Science.* Englewood Cliffs, N.J: Prentice-Hall, 1970.

Butts, D.P. *Teaching Science in the Elementary School.* New York: Free Press, 1973.

Caney, S. *Toy Book.* New York: Workman, 1972.

Carmichael, V. S. *Science Experiences for Young Children.* Los Angeles: Southern California Association for the Education of Young Children, 1969.

Carson, R. *The Sense of Wonder.* New York: Harper & Row, 1965.

"A Child's Garden: A Guide for Parents and Teachers." San Francisco: Public Relations, Chevron Chemical Co., 1974.

Clemons, E. *Shells Are Where You Find Them.* New York: Alfred A. Knopf, 1960.

Cobb, V. *Science Experiments You Can Eat.* Philadelphia: J.B. Lippincott, 1972.

Friedel, A.E. *Teaching Science to Children: The Inquiry Approach Applied.* New York: Random House, 1972.

Goldberg, L. *Children and Science.* New York: Charles E. Scribner's Sons, 1970.

Habben, D. *Science Experiments That Really Work.* Chicago: Follet, 1970.

Holt, B. *Science with Young Children.* Washington, D.C.: National Association for the Education of Young Children, 1977.

Hone, E.B., et al. *A Sourcebook for Elementary Science.* New York: Harcourt Brace & World, 1962.

Hucklesby, S. "Opening Up the Classroom: A Walk Around the School." Urbana, Ill.: ERIC/ECE, 1971.

Lansdown, B., et al. *Teaching Elementary Science: Through Investigation and Colloquium.* New York: Harcourt Brace Jovanovich, 1971.

Mitchell, L.S. *Young Geographer.* New York: Agathon, 1934.

Perryman, L.C. "Science and the Young Child." *Young Children* 20, no. 1 (October 1964): 47-51.

Roche, R.L. *The Child and Science: Wondering, Exploring, Growing.* Washington, D.C.: Association for Childhood Education International, 1977.

Shugure, S.K. *Environmental Education in the Nursery School.* Washington, D.C.: National Science Teachers Association, 1972.

Community Resources

14

The program of the all-day center can be extended and enriched by the use of a variety of community resources. Some of the community organizations and agencies which can be a starting point for activities through which children may pursue their interests are:

YMCA
YWCA
Boys' Clubs
Girls' Clubs
Recreation departments
School music departments
Volunteers from colleges and universities
Dancing classes
Local parks
Girl Scouts
Boy Scouts
Camp Fire Girls
4-H Clubs
Volunteer bureaus to transport children to and from activities
Special interest clubs
Service organizations
Big Brothers
Big Sisters
Public libraries
Children's athletic groups

The child enrolled in an all-day center can participate in any of the after-school activities that any school-age child does. These activities, away from the home and the center, assume increasingly greater importance as children grow older. They provide children with opportunities to learn new things and meet new people. It is especially important for children in an all-day program to play with children other than those enrolled in the center and for center children to feel they are a part of the same kind of after-school activities as their school friends, especially during the summer months. After-school activities away from the center also give children a needed opportunity to be independent and self-sufficient.

Making arrangements for children to go to after-school activities outside the center benefits the child going to the after-school programs and the child who remains at the center. Those remaining have more opportunity for small group activities and for private chats with adult leaders. If the community itself is viewed as an extension of the center, the variety of experiences offered through the center will be limited only by the number of different opportunities in the community and the effectiveness of the staff in finding ways for children to participate.

Several important points must be considered when a center uses community resources to extend and enrich its program. As a first step toward extending the after-school program into the community, the center staff must find out what community resources are available. This means visiting the agencies which offer programs for youth, talking with directors of these programs about whether center children can participate, observing these programs in action, and talking with the parents of the children enrolled. The staff should also establish standards which it feels programs should meet in order for them to be considered. The adequacy of the facility, the quality of the staff and program, how well the programs suit the individual child, should all be considered in deciding whether to support a given program.

Parents must know and understand why the opportunities are being made available to their children. Some parents will be eager to have their children do these things, while other parents may be afraid to have their children leave the center or may think teachers are only trying to lighten their workload. When parents understand the reasons behind these activities and see how their children will benefit, the center staff will generally receive their support—support so necessary for the success of the program.

A number of choices must be available to parents in extending the all-day center program into the community:

1. Parents must be free to decide whether they wish their children to participate. Permission (consent) slips for all activities *must* be secured.

2. Parents may wish to have their children participate in some after-school activities and will make their own arrangements for the activities and the children's transportation.

3. Parents may wish to have their children participate in community after-school program activities with other children from the center and let the center make arrangements for the activities and the children's transportation.

4. Parents may wish to have their children participate in a community after-school program but not want the children to leave the center. For such children, especially in grades one to three, it may be possible for community agencies to offer programs at the center.

Parents and center staff must decide how good the programs are and whether they are right for individual children. Whenever possible, the parent should enroll the child in such programs. If special fees or dues are involved, the parent should be aware of this; center staff may be able to make arrangements for reduced fees in some cases.

Other community resources help families too. Staff should be familiar with whatever is available in the community and be able to judge when families may need help from these agencies. They should know what procedures need to be followed for referrals and what the financial and eligibility requirements of each agency are. Some parents who use day care are struggling with various health, social welfare, legal, and financial problems. The center staff should establish communication with those community agencies which deal with the problems faced by parents.

Some programs have found ways of bringing services to the center through on-site visits and consultation at hours when parents are bringing or picking up their children. Parents are able to meet with a family counselor who can assist them in dealing with their problems or help them find the right agency from which to seek help. Sometimes the family counselor is a center staff member; sometimes community agencies can provide such a service. In either case, parents, children, and the community benefit from liaison between child care staffs and local community agencies.

The following agencies are some which may be helpful in establishing communication.

Family Service Association of America
Jewish Family Service
City Parks and Recreation Department
Visiting Nurses' Association
Catholic Social Service
Child Protective Service Agency
Department of Health Services
Probation Department
Department of Rehabilitation
Community Family Health Centers
Dental Society
Mental Health Centers

Liaison between centers and neighboring elementary schools is especially important. Because the school and center share responsibility for children, open channels of communication should be established and maintained as they respect each other's contribution to the child's life. Many times working parents' schedules prevent them from attending school functions or meeting school personnel firsthand. Center staff can become a bridge between families and the school, interpreting policy decisions, explaining procedures and schedules, and translating sometimes confusing messages relayed by young children. Through such joint efforts, school and child care can supplement each other's important contributions to the lives of children and families.

If the community itself is viewed as an extension of the center, the variety of experiences offered through the center will be limited only by the number of different opportunities in the community and the effectiveness of the staff in finding ways for children to participate.

Staff Meetings: Toward an Effective Program

15

Any or all of the preceding activities can be enriching and interesting in a school-age program; each has been tested and evaluated for children of this age. But each could also be irrelevant, uninteresting, or a waste of time without the adult's understanding of each child, an understanding central to the adult's ability to function well in the center program.

This book began with some brief descriptions of children. They represent confidential information which adults usually learn about children in their centers. A major assumption we have made is that there will be regular, frequent, and searching staff meetings during which adults who interact with the children will exchange information, make interpretations, and attempt to understand the whys and hows of the behaviors they have observed in the children for whom they are responsible.

A weekly staff meeting should be designed to exchange ideas and plans about the program, materials, and activities, and to evaluate completed or ongoing aspects of the program. In addition, there should be observations and information exchanged about individual children and significant events and developments in their lives. In any program where several adults interact with one or more children, it is important not only that they pool their perceptions, but that they agree on what ways of interacting will most enrich the child's well-being and development.

In such a complex program as the one described here, brief daily exchanges can be extremely helpful. Less formal than a staff meeting, but still professional in their focus on growth and development of children and families, such exchanges may involve a teacher and an assistant or the whole center staff. They may last five minutes or fifteen minutes or even longer and must be designed to make the next day at the center pleasant and productive for everyone. When staff members value this kind of professional sharing, they will find time for such meetings early in the morning, after closing, or even during children's naptime. When necessary, staff persons may take over one another's tasks to free individuals for appropriate staff consultation.

While regular staff meetings are imperative, such meetings are difficult to arrange in an all-day child care center. It may be that attendance will vary from meeting to meeting, but with planned communication everyone will have a sense of being part of shared decisions and policies. Some practical suggestions come from experiences of school-age child care center directors.

After most children have left for school—around ten o'clock—there will be a lull which lends itself well to a meeting. It may be important to rotate the time of day when meetings are planned so that different staff members can attend different days and weeks. A staff potluck can provide a welcome chance to socialize and exchange perceptions about children and program, a very necessary aspect of staff planning.

There are differences of opinion regarding staff meetings during paid staff time. Certainly such time is a core aspect of teachers' functioning, and meeting during time for which staff is paid places staff work and planning in its proper, important place. Budgets should reflect this belief about the indispensable nature of staff exchange and planning.

Some centers are able to work out ways of using community resources to enrich their own understanding of children (see Chapter 14). The local Mental Health Association may offer consultation. A professor at a university may be interested in placing fieldwork students in the center for their learning and, in exchange, hold a seminar or provide consultation on particular concerns. Community organizations such as the Family Service Association of America will be pleased to form an alliance out of concern for the same families which they may be serving in different ways. The local public health agencies will be delighted to serve center families and to enter into joint programs with them. Staff meetings may well be organized intermittently to introduce these services and resources to staff members.

All the program activities described in this book will be valuable in direct proportion to the amount of staff thinking and planning which goes on in tune with knowledge about and understanding of the children in the program and their families.

If the program is successful in meeting the needs of the children it serves, we may find:

• That Joseph has become a real leader. He has joined Little League and is getting insistent about the importance of being a good sport. One of the assistant teachers makes time to be alone with Joseph tossing a ball or just talking.

His grandmother became acquainted with other grandmothers and has formed a friendship with the cook at the center. Mrs. T., Joseph's mother, came home to the family in time to visit at the spring open house; she has been encouraged to take a course in child development at the community college.

• That Carrie seems more secure; she has enjoyed some joint family outings arranged by her father, Mr. L., with another center family. Carrie has become friends with a high school girl doing fieldwork at the center; it is like having a big sister.

Mr. L. has talked to the center director about his future plans for his family; the director told him about many community resources.

• That Timothy in his quiet way is somewhat of a leader, too. He organized a way of storing and using sports equipment, and continues to be at home in his three worlds of home, school, and center.

His mother, Mrs. B., has become chairperson of parent meetings and has located interesting speakers from the community, enlarging her own acquaintance with people and activities in the area.

• And that the members of the center staff, seeing all this, recognize their importance in all the lives the center involves.

Index

Acceleration 71
Active play 13-17
  discussion topics 15
  equipment 14-15
  learning opportunities 13-14
  storage 14, 15
  suggestions 15-16
Adults, role of 15, 34
After-school activities away from center
  77-78
Age grouping 6
Agriculture 66, 67
Alfalfa seeds 75
Aluminum foil 23
Animals 74
Ant village 74
Ants on a log 68
Applesauce 67
Aprons 69
Arrivals 9
Art shows 21
Arts and crafts 19-27
  discussion topics 21
  equipment 20-21
  learning opportunities 19-20
  storage 21
  suggestions 21-27
Assessment 15

Backstitch 51, 52
Basting stitch 51, 52
Beads 25
Beanbags 52
Beautician play 36
Bells 74
Birdfeeders 75
  coconut 75
  pine cone 75
  wooden 75
Birds 75

Blocks 29-32, 57
  discussion topics 31
  equipment 30
  learning opportunities 29-30
  storage 30
  suggestions 31-32
Boats
  origami 63
  racing 57
  sailing 63
  walnut shell 63, 75
Bookcases 57
Bookends 23
Bread 68
Breaking the Line 16
Butter 67

Cardboard boxes 36
Careers
  related to construction 31, 57
  related to science 75
  related to water 61
Carpentry—see *woodworking*.
Chalk
  painting 24
  stencil 24
Changes in matter 65, 66, 74
Charcoal 24
Checkers 23
Chemistry 71, 74
Child care centers
  different from school 2
  liaison with community 4, 77-78, 80
  liaison with school 3, 78
  qualities of 5
  role of 1-4
  staff meetings 79-80
  support for parents 2-4, 6, 78, 80
Children, needs of 1-4, 6, 77, 80

Cinnamon toast, painted 68
Circus play 37
Classification 29, 65
Clay
  commercial 21
  dough 22
  flour and salt 22, 25
  plasticine 22
  sawdust 21
Cleanup 9, 11, 19, 59, 65, 66
Climbing structures 15
Cloth, painting on 26
Clothing stores 51
Coconut birdfeeder 75
Coconut shells 47
Collage 21, 22
  wax 22
Colors 21
Community resources 37, 46, 49, 57, 77-78, 80
  and parents 77-78
  importance of 77
  points to consider 77
Competition 11
Concept learning 29-30, 45, 49, 55, 57, 59, 65, 74
Conservation 22, 26, 59, 72, 73
Construction 21-24, 29-32, 57
  careers related to 31, 57
  mobiles 23
  stabiles 23, 26
  with blocks 29-32
  with clay 21-22
  with wire 23
  See also *woodworking*.
Contests 15
Cookies 68
Cooking 65-69
  discussion topics 66-67

equipment 66
  learning opportunities 65-66
  recipes 67-68
  storage 66
  suggestions 67-69
Cook's hat 68
Cooperation 11, 19, 21, 29, 33, 37, 39, 55, 72
Costumes 37, 41, 49, 51
Crafts—see *arts and crafts*.
Crayons
  etchings 24
  melted 24
  rubbings 24
  stencil 24
Creative dramatics—see *dramatic play*.
Creative movement—see *dance*.
Creativity 19, 21, 23, 34, 36, 41, 45, 46, 59, 75
Cupcake ice cream cones 68
Current events 36

Dams 61
Dance 13, 15, 43-47
  discussion topics 44-45
  equipment 44
  folk dances 15, 43, 45
  learning opportunities 43-44
  storage 44
  suggestions 45-46
Departures 9
Desserts 67, 68
Discussion topics
  active play 15
  arts and crafts 21
  blocks 31
  cooking 66-67
  dance 44-45
  dramatic play 36
  gardening 73-74

knitting 50-51
mud play 61
music activities 44-45
nature activities 73-74
puppets 40
sand play 61
science activities 73-74
sewing 50-51
water play 61
weaving 50-51
woodworking 56
Dollhouses 57
Donuts 68
Dough clays 22
Dramatic play 29, 33-38, 56
   discussion topics 36
   equipment 34, 36, 37
   learning opportunities 33-34
   storage 36
   suggestions 36-37
   with blocks 29
   See also *puppets.*
Drum beaters 47
Drums 45, 47
Dyes 26, 51

Easels 26
Eating—see *mealtimes.*
Economics 31, 66
Eggs 74
   friendly egghead 75
Electricity 73, 75
Energy 71, 73
Equipment
   active play 14-15
   arts and crafts 20-21
   blocks 30
   cooking 66
   dance 44
   dramatic play 34, 36, 37
   gardening 72
   knitting 50
   mud play 59
   music activities 44
   nature activities 72
   puppets 39-40, 41
   sand play 59
   science activities 72
   sewing 50
   water play 59
   weaving 50
   woodworking 55-56
Esthetics 20, 27, 29, 40, 45, 49, 65
Etching, crayon 24
Evaluation of program 79
Experiences as bases for dramatic play 36

Families—see *parents.*
Family play 34
Finger paints 24-25
   monoprints 25
Firefighter play 36
First aid 14, 56
Flour and salt clay 22, 25
Flowers 74
Folk dances 15, 43, 45
Food—see *cooking.*
Footstools 23
Force 71
Friction 71
Fruit treats, frozen 67
Funnel cakes 68

Gadget boards 74
Games 13, 15-16
   Breaking the Line 16
   I Spy 16
   Lemonade 16
   Over and Under 16
   Run, Sheep, Run 16
   What Did I Do? 16
   Wiggle Waggle 16
Gardening 65, 71-76
   discussion topics 73-74
   equipment 72
   learning opportunities 72
   storage 72-73
   suggestions 74-75
Gas station play 36
Grasses 73
Grooming—see *personal habits.*

Hammers 56
Hand-eye coordination, 21, 29, 39, 49, 55, 59, 65
Hat 52
   for cooks 68
Health 9, 11, 13, 65
Herbs 74

I Spy 16
Improvisation 33-34
Indian play 37
Indoor activities 6, 7, 8
Inks 24, 26
Insects 74

Jewelry 25
Jingle sticks 47

Knitting 49-53
   discussion topics 50-51
   equipment 50
   learning opportunities 49

storage 50, 51
suggestions 51-52

Language skills 11, 19, 21, 29, 31, 33, 39, 43, 49, 55, 59, 61, 65, 66, 67, 72
Leaf prints 26, 74
Learning opportunities
   active play 13-14
   arts and crafts 19-20
   blocks 29-30
   cooking 65-66
   dance 43-44
   dramatic play 33-34
   gardening 71-72
   knitting 49
   mud play 59
   music activities 43-44
   nature activities 71-72
   puppets 39
   routines 9-11
   sand play 59
   science activities 71-72
   sewing 49
   water play 59
   weaving 49
   woodworking 55
Leather crafts 25-26
Lemonade 16
Liaison
   between center and community 4, 77-78, 80
   between center and school, 3, 78
Looms 51

Machines 73, 74
Macrame 51
Magnets 71, 73, 74
Marionettes—see *puppets.*
Mathematical concepts 11, 29, 31, 49, 55, 65, 66, 74
Mealtimes 9, 10, 65
Measurements 74
Mechanical parts 37
Medical play 34
Mobiles 23
Monoprints 24, 25
Mosaics 27
Movement activities—see *active play; dance.*
Mud play 59-63
   discussion topics 61
   equipment 59
   learning opportunities 59
   storage 61
   suggestions 62-63
Mud, properties of 62

Multicultural experiences 20, 21, 43, 45, 51, 65-66
Muscle coordination 13, 19, 29, 39, 49, 55, 59, 65
Music activities 13, 15, 43-47
   discussion topics 44-45
   equipment 44
   learning opportunities 43-44
   storage 44
   suggestions 45-47
Musical instruments 37, 43-44, 45, 46-47
   coconut shells 47
   drum beaters 47
   drums 45, 47
   jingle sticks 47
   rhythm sticks 45, 46
   shaker bells 47
   sound shakers 46
   tambourines 45, 47
   tapping rhythm instruments 47

Nature activities 26, 71-76
   discussion topics 73-74
   equipment 72
   learning opportunities 71-72
   storage 72-73
   suggestions 74-75
Newspapers 26, 27, 68
Nutrition 65, 66

Obstacle course 15
Office play 34
Old Masters Printing 24
Origami boats 63
Outdoor activities 6, 7, 8
Over and Under 16
Overcast stitch 51, 52

Painting 21, 24-25, 26
   chalk 24
   enamel 26
   finger 24-26
   ink 26
   spatter 26
   straw 26
   string 26
   tempera 26
   water color 26
Pantomime 16, 33, 46
Paper 26-27
   mosaics 27
   papier-mâché 26-27
   plates 27
   sculpture 27
Papier-mâché 26-27
Parents
   expectations for children 1, 2-4

involvement 2-4, 5, 6, 21, 37, 43, 67, 77-78
  meetings 5, 9
  support for 5, 6, 78
Peanut butter balls 67
Pencils 24
Pens, felt 24
Permission slips 77, 78
Personal habits 9, 11, 59
Photography 31
Physical development—see *active play; dance.*
Physics 71
Pianos 45
Picnics 10, 65, 66
Pigs in blankets 68
Pine cone birdfeeder 75
Planes 56
Plants 73
Plaster of paris 27
Plasticine 22
Politics 31
Poetry 36, 40, 45
Pot holders 51
Potatoes 75
Props 36, 37, 41, 45, 56
Pudding-wiches 68
Puppets 36, 39-41, 51, 56, 57
  discussion topics 40
  equipment 39-40, 41
  learning opportunities 39
  storage 40, 41
  suggestions 41
  theater 36, 41, 57

Racing boats 57
Recipes
  ants on a log 68
  applesauce 67
  bread 68
  cinnamon toast, painted 68
  cookies 68
  cupcake ice cream cones 68
  donuts 68
  fruit treats, frozen 67
  funnel cakes 68
  peanut butter balls 67
  pigs in blankets 68
  pudding-wiches 68
Record players 45
Relay games 15, 16
Repairs 57
Responsibility 11, 36, 49, 55, 72
Rest times 9, 10
Rhythm sticks 45, 46

Rockets 74
Rocks 74
Routines 9-11
  arrivals 9
  cleanup 9, 11
  departures 9
  learning opportunities 9-11
  mealtimes 9, 10
  personal habits 9, 11
  rest times 9, 10
  tips for handling 11
"Rube Goldberg" machines 74
Rules 15
Run, Sheep, Run 16
Running stitch 51, 52

Safety 14, 15, 21, 30, 31, 36, 49, 51, 55, 56, 59, 61, 66, 73
Sailboats 63
Sand play 59-63
  discussion topics 61
  equipment 59
  learning opportunities 59
  storage 61
  suggestions 62-63
Sand, properties of 62
Sandbox 62
Sandpaper 56
Sawdust modeling clay 22
Sawhorses 37
Saws 56
Schedules 5-8
  school year 5, 7
  vacations and holidays 6, 8
Science activities 71-76
  careers related to 75
  discussion topics 73-74
  equipment 72
  learning opportunities 71-72
  storage 72-73
  suggestions 74-75
Scrapbooks 45, 75
Scribble-Scrabbles 24
Sculpture
  paper 27
  plaster of paris 27
  soap 27
  sticks 27
  wire 23
Seaweed 74
Seeds 73, 74, 75
Self-reliance 11, 13
Sensory experiences 15, 45, 65, 71, 73, 74
Sewing 49-53
  discussion topics 50-51
  equipment 50

  learning opportunities 49
  storage 50, 51
  suggestions 51-52
Sewing machines 51
Shadows 74
Shaker bells 47
Shape 29
Shuttles 51
Sight 65, 73
Sit-upons 51
Skill-building 15
Slip stitch 52
Smell 65, 73
Snacks, ideas for 67-68
Snacktimes—see *mealtimes.*
Soap 27
Soil 73, 74
Sound 45, 65, 71, 73, 74
Sound shakers 46
Spaceships 37
Spatial concepts 29, 45
Spatter painting 26
Sprouts 75
Stabiles 23, 26
Staff meetings 79-80
Stencils 24
Sticks 27
Stitchery—see *sewing.*
Stitches 51-52
Storage 14, 15, 21, 30, 31, 36, 40, 41, 44, 50, 51, 56, 61, 66, 72-73
Store play 36
Straw painting 26
String painting 26
Suggestions
  active play 15-16
  arts and crafts 21-27
  blocks 31-32
  cooking 67-69
  dance 45-46
  dramatic play 36-37
  gardening 74-75
  knitting 51-52
  mud play 62-63
  music activities 45-47
  nature activities 74-75
  puppets 41
  sand play 62-63
  science activities 74-75
  sewing 51-52
  water play 62-63
  weaving 51-52
  woodworking 56-57
Swimming 61, 62

Tambourines 45, 47

Tapping rhythm instruments 47
Taste 65, 66, 73
Teams 15
Television 6
Time 65
Tires 37, 62
Tools, proper use of 21
Touch 65, 73
Touching boxes 74
Trampolines 37
Transportation play 36
Treehouses 37
Trips 21, 27, 31, 36, 41, 44, 45, 51, 57, 61, 67, 74, 75

Wall hangings 23, 51
Walnut shell boats 43, 75
Washing—see *personal habits.*
Water
  as natural resource 59, 61
  careers related to 61
  conservation of 59, 61, 62
  pollution 61
  properties of 61, 62
Water play 59-63
  discussion topics 61
  equipment 59
  learning opportunities 59
  storage 61
  suggestions 62-63
Waterfall 62-63
Wax collage 22
Weather 67, 73
Weaving 49-53
  discussion topics 50-51
  equipment 50
  learning opportunities 49
  storage 50, 51
  suggestions 51-52
What Did I Do? 16
Wheels 73
Whipstitch 51
Wiggle Waggle 16
Wigs 37
Wire sculpture 23
Wooden birdfeeder 75
Woodworking 31, 55-58
  careers related to 31, 57
  discussion topics 56
  equipment 55-56
  learning opportunities 55
  storage 56
  suggestions 56-57
Worm farm 74

Yarn 51

Selected NAEYC Publications

Code #	Title	Price
303	A Beginner's Bibliography, by Bernice H. Fleiss	$ .50
200	Better Day Care for the Young Child Through a Merged Governmental and Nongovernmental Effort, by Cornelia Goldsmith	$5.00
132	The Block Bood, edited by Elisabeth S. Hirsch	$3.50
213	Caring: Supporting Children's Growth, by Rita M. Warren	$2.00
127	The Cognitively Oriented Curriculum: A Framework for Preschool Teachers, by David P. Weikart, Linda Rogers, Carolyn Adcock, and Donna McClelland	$3.50
402S	Cómo Reconocer un Buen Porgrama de Educación Pre-Escolar	$ .25
119	Curriculum Is What Happens: Planning Is the Key, edited by Laura L. Dittmann	$2.00
300	Early Childhood Education: An Introduction to the Profession, by James L. Hymes, Jr.	$1.50
110	Early Childhood Education: It's an Art? It's a Science? edited by J. D. Andrews	$4.00
108	Education for Parenting, by Mary B. Lane	$3.00
302	A Guide to Discipline, by Jeannette Galambos Stone	$1.50
210	The Idea Box, by Austin AEYC	$5.75
304	Ideas That Work With Young Children, edited by Katherine Read Baker	$3.00
130	Imagination: Key to Human Potential, by Polly McVicar	$3.50
101	Let's Play Outdoors, by Katherine Read Baker	$1.00
308	Mud, Sand, and Water, by Dorothy M. Hill	$2.00
109	One Child Indivisible, edited by J. D. Andrews	$5.25

135   Parent Involvement in Early Childhood Education, by Alice S. Honig $3.00

102   Piaget, Children, and Number, by Constance Kamii and Rheta DeVries $2.00

115   Planning Environments for Young Children: Physical Space, by Sybil Kritchevsky
and Elizabeth Prescott with Lee Walling $1.75

123   Play and Playgrounds, by Jeannette Galambos Stone $3.25

306   Play as a Learning Medium, edited by Doris Sponseller $2.75

129   Play: The Child Strives Toward Self-Realization, edited by Georgianna Engstrom $2.50

126   Promoting Cognitive Growth: A Developmental-Interaction Point of View, by Barbara
Biber, Edna Shapiro, David Wickens in collaboration with Elizabeth Gilkeson $2.75

307   Providing the Best for Young Children, edited by Jan McCarthy and Charles R. May . $3.25

309   Science with Young Children, by Bess-Gene Holt $3.25

128   The Significance of the Young Child's Motor Development, edited by Georgianna
Engstrom $2.25

402E   Some Ways of Distinguishing a Good Early Childhood Program................... $ .25

310   Talks with Teachers, by Lilian G. Katz.. $3.00

311   Teaching Practices: Reexamining Assumptions, edited by Bernard Spodek............ $2.25

Order from NAEYC
      1834 Connecticut Avenue, N.W.
      Washington, DC 20009

For information about these and other NAEYC publications, write for a free publications brochure.

Please enclose full payment for orders under $10.00.